Geography Matters

FOUNDATION

Series Editor:

John Hopkin

Editor:

Andy Leeder, Copleston High School, Ipswich

Authors:

Nicola Arber, Bournville School, Birmingham

Rob Bowden, Development Education Centre, Birmingham

Lisa James, Cockshut Hill School, Birmingham

Sue Lomas, Henbury High School, Macclesfield

Garrett Nagle, St Edward's School, Oxford

Roger Sanders, Sir John Talbot's School, Whitchurch

Linda Thompson, formerly at Sandbach School, Sandbach

Paul Thompson, Ounsdale High School, Wolverhampton

Heinemann Educational Publishers
Halley Court, Jordan Hill, Oxford, OX2 8EJ
a division of Reed Educational & Professional Publishing Ltd
Heinemann is a registered trademark of Reed Educational & Professional Publishing Ltd

OXFORD MELBOURNE AUCKLAND
JOHANNESBURG BLANTYRE GABORONE
IBADAN PORTSMOUTH NH (USA) CHICAGO

© Nicola Arber, Rob Bowden, Lisa James, Sue Lomas, Garrett Nagle, Roger Sanders, Linda Thompson, Paul Thompson, 2002

Copyright notice
All rights reserved. No part of this publication may be reproduced in any material form (including photocopying or storing it in any medium by electronic means and whether or not transiently or incidentally to some other use of this publication) without the prior written permission of the copyright owner, except in accordance with the provisions of the Copyright, Designs and Patents Act 1988 or under the terms of a licence issued by the Copyright Licensing Agency Ltd, 90 Tottenham Court Road, London W1P 0LP. Applications for the copyright owner's written permission to reproduce any part of this publication should be addressed to the publisher.

First published 2002

ISBN 0 435 35525 2

06 05 04 03 02
10 9 8 7 6 5 4 3 2 1

Designed and illustrated by Gecko Ltd, Bicester, Oxon, Tokay, Roger Penwill, John Storey, and Geoff Ward
Original illustrations © Heinemann Educational Publishers 2001
Printed and bound in Spain by Edelvives

Acknowledgements
The authors and publishers would like to thank the following for permission to reproduce copyright material.

Photos
p. 4 *A* Panos Pictures/A. le Garsmeur, *B* Panos Pictures/Rob Cousins, *C* Robert Harding/Doug Traverso, *D:* Popperfoto/Reuters/Rafiqur Rahman, *E:* Science Photo Library/Ted Kerasote; **p. 5** *F* Woodfall Wild Images/Nigel Hicks, *G* Robert Harding/C. Bowman, *H* Hutchison Library/Ian Lloyd; **p. 6** Hutchison Library/Crispin Hughes; **p. 7** Still Pictures/David Drain; **p. 8** *A:* Panos Pictures/Betty Press, *B:* Robert Harding/Brian Harrison; **p. 10** Panos Pictures/Jon Spaull; **p. 15** EASI Images/Rob Bowden; **p. 16** EASI Images/Rob Bowden; **p.18** Panos Pictures/Jeremy Hartley; **p. 20** *A* Science Photo Library/Ted Kerasote, *B:* Robert Harding Picture Library; **p. 22** *A* Robert Harding/Explorer, *B:* Still Pictures, *C:* Spectrum Colour Library; **p. 24** *A:* Still Pictures/Pierre Gleizes, *B:* World Pictures, *C:* Spectrum Colour Library/P. Thompson; **p. 25** *D:* World Pictures, *E* Robert Harding Picture Library/S. Harris, *F* Robert Harding Picture Library/C. Martin; **p. 26** *A* Still Pictures/Patrick Bertrand, *B* Magnum Photos/Gilles Peress, *C* Spectrum Colour Library; **p. 28** *B* Still Pictures/Klein/Hubert, *A* Robert Harding Picture Library; **p. 30** *Top L:* Spectrum Colour Library, *R:* Eyewire **p. 34** Woodfall Wild Images/Bob Gibbons; **p. 35** Environmental Images/Oliver Waterlow; **p. 36** *C:* Science Photo Library, *D:* Still Pictures/J.F. Mutzig, *E:* Still Pictures/Pierre Gleizes; **p. 37** Oxford Scientific Films/Raymond Blythe; **p. 38** Robert Harding Picture Library/E. Simanor; **p. 40** Corbis; **p. 44** Advertising Archives; **p. 45** *B:* Associated Press/Richard Vogel, *C:* Popperfoto/Paolo Cocco/Reuters; **p. 52** Nike; **p. 60** *A* Still Pictures/Mark Edwards, *B* Spectrum Colour Library, *C:* Hutchison Picture Library/Nigel Sitwell, *D* Spectrum Colour Library, *E:* World Pictures, *F:* Spectrum Colour Library; *G:* Spectrum Colour Library, **p. 64** Skyscan; **p. 66** World Pictures; **p. 73** *top R:* Science Photo Library/Worldsat International and J. Knighton, *middle L:* Science Photo Library/Julian Baum & David Angus; **p. 74** Eye Ubiquitous/Paul Thompson; **p. 75** Robert Harding Picture Library/Adam Woolfitt; **p. 76** *A:* Spectrum Colour Library, *B:* The Art Archive/Musée Guimet Paris/Dagli Orti; **p. 77** Corbis; **p. 78** *B* Robert Harding Picture Library/Tony Waltham, *C:* Robert Harding Picture Library/Gina Corrigan, *D:* Picture Works/Ingrid Booz Morejohn; **p. 79** *E* Associated Press/Greg Baker, *F:* Associated Press/Zhou Wenguang, **p. 81** Spectrum Colour Library; **p. 82** *top R:* Robert Harding Picture Library/Gavin Hellier, *top L:* Spectrum Colour Library, *bottom:* Corbis/Steve Kaufmal; **p. 83** *top R:* Magnum Photos, Still Pictures/Francois Suchel; **p. 85** *top L:* Rex Features/IWASA, *middle R:* Associated Press/David Guttenfelder, *bottom L:* Science Photo Library/NASA; **p. 87** *top L:* Robert Harding Picture Library/Chester Beatty Library, *middle R:* James Davis Travel Photography, *bottom R:* Eye Ubiquitous/Frank Leather; **p. 88** Associated Press/Zxinhua; **p. 89** Picture Works/Ingrid Booz Morejohn; **p. 90** Mitsubishi Electric Europe; **p. 91** Spectacular China; **p. 92** *C:* & **p. 70** *C* Eye Ubiquitous/Nick Bonetti; **p. 92** *D:* & **p. 70** *D:* Eye Ubiquitous/Chris Fairclough; **p. 92** *E:* & **p. 71** *F* Spectrum Colour Library; **p. 92** *F:* & **p. 71** *E:* Robert Harding Picture Library/Nigel Blythe; **p. 92** *G:* & **p. 71** *G:* Robert Harding Picture Library; **p. 92** *H* and **p. 71** *H* Still Pictures/Hartmut Schwarzbach; **p. 94** Dr Jurg Alean/Stromboli; **p. 97** *top:* Spectrum Colour Library, *bottom:* Corbis/Mike Zens; **p. 99** *L:* Popperfoto/Reuters, *R:* Rex Features/Sipa Press; **p. 102** Dr Jurg Alean/Stromboli; **p. 103** Science Photo Library/David Parker; **p. 106** *L:* Earthquake Hazard Centre/Rajendra Desai, *R:* Hutchison Picture Library/Bernard Regent; **p. 108** *middle L:* Rex Features/Nils Jorgensen, *middle R:* AP Photos/Findlay Kember, *bottom L:* Still Pictures/Klaus Andrews; **p. 110** *top L:* Getmapping.com, *bottom L:* BMW AG; **p. 112** Garrett Nagle; **p. 113** *middle R:* Chris Honeywell, *top R:* Garrett Nagle; **p. 114** *middle R:* BMW AG, *bottom L:* BMW AG; **p. 115** BMW AG; **p. 118** Get Mapping; **p. 120** Paul Thompson; **p. 123** Paul Thompson; **p. 128** Science Photo Library/Dr. Jeremy Burgess; **p. 129** *top R:* Still Pictures/Fred Dott, *top L:* Environmental Images/S. Mahoney; **p. 130** *A:* Science Photo Library/Microfield Scientific Ltd., *B:* Still Pictures/Roland Birke, *C:* Oxford Scientific Films/Paul Kay, *D:* Oxford Scientific Films/Sue Scott, *E:* Still Pictures/J.P. Sylvestre, *F:* Woodfall Wild Images/Mark Hamblin, *G:* Woodfall Wild Images/Tom Campbell, *H:* Woodfall Wild Images/Bill Coster; **p. 134** Axiom/Jonathan Renouf; **p. 135** *middle R:* Greenpeace, *bottom R:* Science Photo Library/Tom McHugh; **p. 136** *E:* Still Pictures/Klaus Andrews, *F* Robert Harding Picture Library, *G:* Science Photo Library/NASA; **p. 137** Science Photo Library/Simon Fraser, *J* Environmental Images/Martin Bond, *top R:* Still Pictures/Hartmut Schwarzbach; **p. 138** Greenpeace; **p. 139** *O:* Oxford Scientific Films/Colin Monteath, *P:* Panos Pictures/Fred Hoogervorst.

Text, Maps and Diagrams
p. 6 Source C ActionAid *Fighting Poverty Together, ActionAid's Strategy* 1999–2003; **p. 77 Source C** (1/12/2000, 20/5/2001) *The Daily Telegraph* **p. 56** DFID, *Making globalisation work for the world's poor: an introduction to the UK Government's White Paper on International Development 2000*; **p. 20 Source C** Forestry Stewardship Council A.C; **p. 50 Source C** (Andrew Osborne 23/11/2000) *The Guardian* **p. 63 Source E** *The Guardian* web site; **p. 77 Source C** (3/4/2001, 15/5/2001, 13/6/2001) *The Guardian*; **p. 65 Source A, p. 112, Sources A, B, 119 Source D** Maps reproduced from Ordnance Survey mapping with the permission of the Controller of Her Majesty's Stationery Office, ©Crown Copyright. All rights reserved. Licence No. 10000230; **p. 77** Source C (12/9/2000, 5/4/2001) *The Times*; **p. 6 Source B, 9 Source C,** United Nations Development Programme, *Human Development Report* 1999; **p.12 Source B, 81 Source B** United Nations Human Development Index 1998; **p.14 Source A, 17 Source B, 56 Sources A, B** United Nations Development Programme 1999; **p. 17 Source B** United Nations Development Programme 2000 and (1996) UNICEF; **p. 7 Source F** *Western Mail*; **p. 68 Source A** (Spring 1999) *Which* Magazines; **p. 6 Source D** World Bank *World Development Report* 1999; **p. 12 Source A** (1998) World Bank; **p. 20 Source D** World Commission on Environment and Development *Our Common Future* 1987

The publishers have made every effort to trace the copyright holders, but if they have inadvertently overlooked any, they will be pleased to make the necessary arrangements at the first opportunity.

Throughout the book these symbols are used with activities that use literacy, numeracy and ICT skills.

Contents

Websites The authors have provided a list of topic-linked
websites for the use alongside *Geography Matters 3, Foundation*
which can be found at www.heinemann.co.uk/hotlinks.
Please insert the code 5252P at the website to access them.

1 What is development?

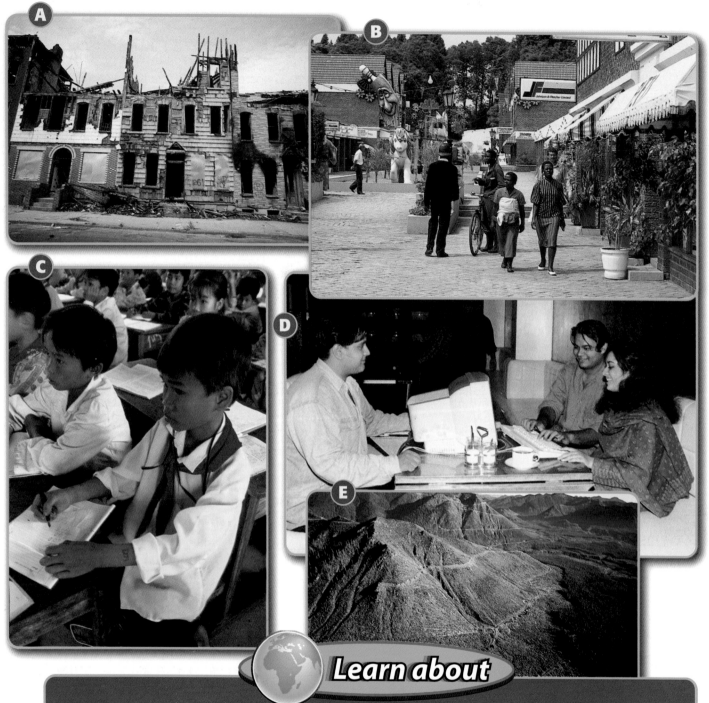

A

B

C

D

E

Learn about

Development affects us all, but in very different ways. For some it can bring great benefits, such as better jobs or improved health, but for others it brings little change in their day-to-day lives and may even make things worse. In this unit you will explore what development means and you will learn:

⑥ what development means to different people

⑥ what development means in your local area

⑥ how patterns of development vary globally

⑥ how different parts of the world are connected by development

⑥ how geographers analyse data to understand development

⑥ who benefits and who loses as a result of development

⑥ what 'sustainable development' means

⑥ what governments and others do to help development.

Perceptions of development

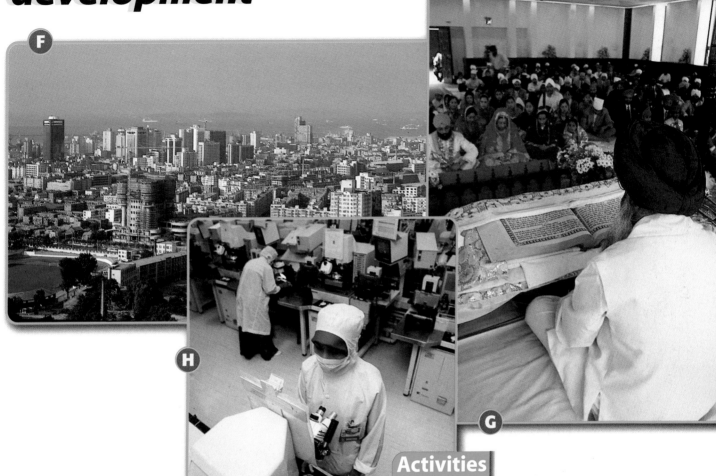

Getting Technical

⊚ **Perception:** how different people see the world. If someone smiles, your perception might be that they are happy. Perception is important to geographers because different people can see the same place or event in different ways.

⊚ **MEDCs** (More Economically Developed Countries): wealthy and industrialised nations. They include those from North America and Western Europe and Australia, New Zealand and Japan. They are also known as *Industrialised Countries*, *Developed Countries*, *The North* or *The First World*.

⊚ **LEDCs** (Less Economically Developed Countries): usually poorer and more agricultural nations. Many of these countries are in Central and South America, Africa and Asia. They are also known as *Developing Countries*, *The South* or *The Third World*.

Activities

Discussion activity

1 With a partner, look at the eight photographs on these pages.

   a Select four photographs and describe to your partner what they show.

   b Now let your partner describe the remaining photographs.

2 **a** Which of the photographs show life in more developed places (MEDCs) and which photographs show life in less developed places (LEDCs)? The locations are shown on page 23 – but don't cheat!

   b Did any of the photographs give you problems when you were putting them into the two groups? Discuss the problems with your teacher.

3 After a class discussion, write down what you think 'Development' means.

4 Start a word bank for this unit with the key words you have used so far. 📖

5

Views of development

People think about development in many different ways. Their viewpoints will depend on their own situations and experiences of development. Think about these differing definitions and views of development.

A Development for me is being able to educate my children and keep them healthy so that they have greater opportunities to earn money and have a better life than me.

(Fisherman, Lake Victoria, Uganda, 1999)

B United Nations Development Programme (from *Human Development Report*, 1999)

The real wealth of a nation is its people. And the purpose of development is to create an environment for people to enjoy long, healthy and creative lives.

C ActionAid (adapted from *Fighting Poverty Together: ActionAid's Strategy 1999–2003*)

The world is not an equal place. The world's resources are not being being shared out in a fair way – we must do something about this! If we do, we have a chance to wipe out poverty.

D World Bank (adapted from *World Development Report*, 1999)

Development means raising incomes but it means much more. People should be given better health services and educational opportunities. They should be given a clean environment to live in.

Activities

1. Look at the opinions given in **A** – **D** above. Some words are mentioned several times.

Find the words below	Write down the number of times each word is mentioned
Poverty	
Education	
Health	
Long life	
Fair	
Money / Income / Wealth	

2. Go back to the writing you did when you attempted exercise 3 on page 5.

   a Have your ideas of development changed?

   b Add any new ideas to your writing.

3. Add any new words to your word bank for this unit.

Development is not just about global changes and the well-being of whole countries – it involves your own neighbourhood too. Sometimes development can affect your neighbourhood more directly – for example, there may be plans to build a new road or to close a nearby mine or factory. The newspaper cuttings in **F** are about the development of wind farms in Mid Wales.

Mind blowing

A good night's sleep is just a dream for inhabitants of a once delightful rural Welsh village. The constant drone of twenty new turbines is driving them to distraction. Windmills, they say, have ruined their lives.

Plea for balance in wind farm debate

Wind farms are generally highly visible, and they are sometimes more noisy than they should be. But they are the most energy-efficient of all the electricity generating technologies.

" Wind farm power is unreliable. Wind farms with their tiny and unreliable power production can never replace power stations. "

£11m wind farm project breezes in

The start of a £11m wind farm project in Mid Wales will provide power for 7000 homes. The managing director of National Wind Power said: 'It will mean a further input of work to the local community and at the same time make a large and positive contribution to the environment.'

Blowing away wind farm myths

… electricity made using coal contributes to global warming and to acid rain, which continues to cause widespread damage throughout Wales. Wind energy, on the other hand, is pollution-free.

'These awful things could destroy the beauty and quietness of the Welsh countryside when it's covered in these dreadful propellors.'

'Our house is unsellable.'

F Views on wind farm development taken from the *Western Mail*

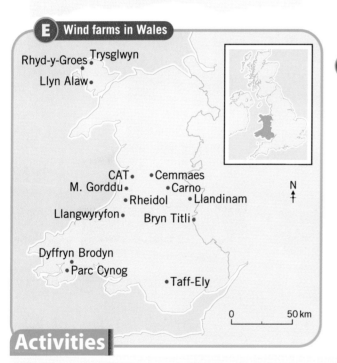

E Wind farms in Wales

Rhyd-y-Groes· ·Trysglwyn
Llyn Alaw·

CAT· ·Cemmaes
M. Gorddu· ·Carno
·Rheidol ·Llandinam
Llangwyryfon· Bryn Titli·

Dyffryn Brodyn
·Parc Cynog

·Taff-Ely

N
↑

0   50 km

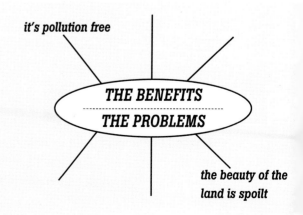

G A wind farm at Llandinam, Wales

Activities

1. Draw a spider diagram to show the benefits of wind farm development (the good points) and the problems they might cause (the bad things). One example has been given on each side of the diagram to help you get started.

2. **a** In your class, discuss a local issue which affects your own community. Try to find information about the issue in your local newspaper.

   b Draw a spider diagram like the one in activity **1** to show the benefits and the problems resulting from the issue.

it's pollution free

THE BENEFITS

THE PROBLEMS

the beauty of the land is spoilt

Development and quality of life

A Village on Lake Volta, Ghana

B Rush hour on London bridge

The quality of life enjoyed by individuals depends greatly on whether they live in a more or less developed country. In the UK, for example, a child born today can expect to live for around 77 years, to attend school and to have enough food to eat. But a child born today in Kenya can expect to live to just 52, has only a 68 per cent chance of completing primary school and a 59 per cent chance of regularly getting enough food to eat. People living in more developed countries generally enjoy a better quality of life than people in less developed countries, as shown in table **C**.

Getting Technical ▾

ⓖ **Standard of living** is used to describe how wealthy people are. Those with greater wealth are thought to have a higher standard of living than those with less money.

ⓖ **Quality of life** is the way people can live their daily lives, not just how poor or wealthy they are. Do they have enough to eat? Can they afford to educate their children? Do they have shelter at night?

Region of the world	Life expectancy (years)	Under-five mortality rate (per thousand)	Adult literacy rate (%)	GNP per capita (US $)
Sub-Saharan Africa	49	172	58.5	530
Arab States	66	72	59.7	2 200
East Asia	70	46	83.4	1 140
South-East Asia	66	57	88.2	1 130
South Asia	63	106	54.3	490
Latin America and the Caribbean	69	39	87.7	3 830
Eastern Europe and former USSR	69	33	98.6	2 100
Industrialised countries	76	14	97.4	20 900
World	67	84	78.8	4 910

Data taken from UNDP Human Development Report 1999

C Key variations in quality of life by region, 1998

Activities

1. Use an atlas to find the countries where photographs **A** and **B** were taken.

2. **a** Draw a Development Compass Rose (DCR) as shown in **D** in the centre of a large sheet of paper.

   b Look carefully at images **A** and **B**. Draw part of each image at each point of the compass to show that you understand the meaning of:

   Ⓢ Natural   Ⓢ Social

   Ⓢ Economic   Ⓢ Who decides?

   Ask your teacher for some ideas.

3. Look at table **C**. Explain why you might prefer to live in Industrialised Countries (for example Britain) compared to countries in Sub-Saharan Africa.

4. **Extension**

   a Imagine what a typical day might be like for people shown in photographs **A** and **B**. Write a diary entry for someone in each photograph.

   b Compare the photographs again. Which place might you prefer to live in, and why?

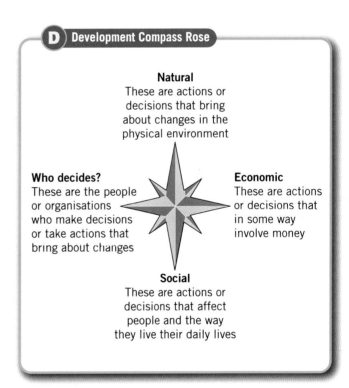

D Development Compass Rose

Natural
These are actions or decisions that bring about changes in the physical environment

Who decides?
These are the people or organisations who make decisions or take actions that bring about changes

Economic
These are actions or decisions that in some way involve money

Social
These are actions or decisions that affect people and the way they live their daily lives

Regional variations in development

A Rio de Janeiro, Brazil

Differences in quality of life can also be found *within* countries – people in more and less developed countries can sometimes share a similar quality of life. For example, homeless people living in the UK may have much in common with people in less developed countries. Similarly, wealthy business owners or managers living in Kenya may enjoy a quality of life as good as that of people living in more developed countries, or even better. Geographers call these differences **inequalities** and, as you have seen, they can be studied at any scale from global to local.

Activities

1. Look at photograph **A** and discuss the inequalities that people living here might experience.
2. List the inequalities that can be seen in your own community. Find or take a photograph and label it to show these inequalities.
3. Using your ideas from questions **1** and **2**, brainstorm what might cause such inequalities. Draw a spider diagram to record your thoughts. Start your diagram with 'Causes of inequality' in the centre box.
4. Good geographers should look for linkages between different causes, as well as for individual causes. Try to make some linkages in your spider diagram. For example, lack of education often makes it harder to find employment, so 'poor education' and 'unemployment' could be linked by an arrow.

help!

Not all of your ideas are necessarily linked. Others could have several links or be linked in both directions. Think carefully before you mark on the linkages.

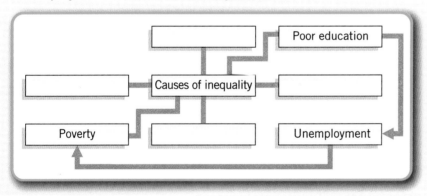

Getting Technical ▼

⑤ **Gross National Product (GNP):** The value of the goods and services produced by a country and the income it earns from overseas. This is measured in US dollars (US $). It is often divided by the population to produce a measure called *GNP per capita*.

⑤ **Human Development Index (HDI):** The HDI is used by the United Nations Development Programme (UNDP) to measure development. It is worked out by combining three different indicators: life expectancy, education levels, and income per person. The HDI has a value between 0 and 1 – a higher value means a higher level of human development.

Mapping development

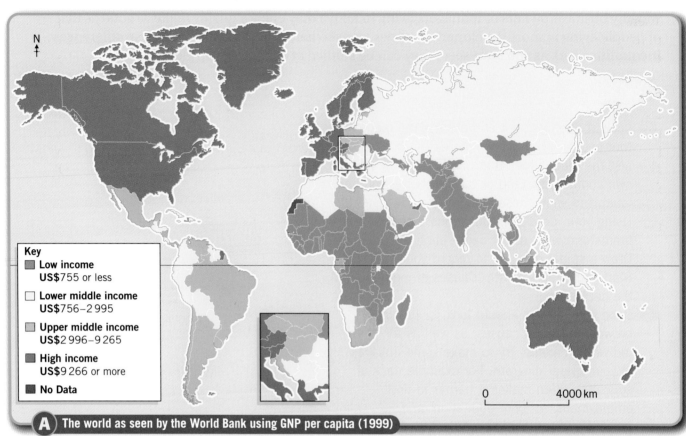

Key

- ■ **Low income**
  US$755 or less
- □ **Lower middle income**
  US$756–2 995
- ▨ **Upper middle income**
  US$2 996–9 265
- ▨ **High income**
  US$9 266 or more
- ■ **No Data**

0   4000 km

A The world as seen by the World Bank using GNP per capita (1999)

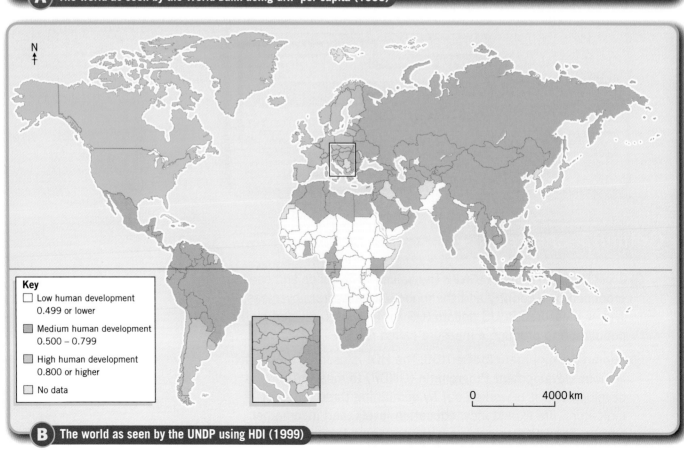

Key

- □ **Low human development**
  0.499 or lower
- ▨ **Medium human development**
  0.500 – 0.799
- ▨ **High human development**
  0.800 or higher
- □ **No data**

0   4000 km

B The world as seen by the UNDP using HDI (1999)

Measuring development

There are many different ways of measuring how developed a country is. Geographers call these **development indicators**.

The World Bank measures development using Gross National Product (GNP) per capita. It uses this measure to divide the world into four different groups of countries: low income, lower-middle income, upper-middle income and high income. According to this method, Luxembourg was the most developed country and Ethiopia the least developed in 1999. Map **A** on page 12 shows how the World Bank views the world.

The United Nations Development Programme (UNDP) uses the Human Development Index (HDI) to measure development. Using the HDI, the UNDP divides the world into three groups of countries: low, medium and high human development. By this measure, Norway was the most developed country and Sierra Leone the least developed in 1999. Map **B** shows how the world looks when measured using the HDI.

Activities

1. Ask your teacher for a large map of the world. It would be helpful if the boundaries of countries are shown.

   a In this section of the book, Norway and Luxembourg are said to be most developed – find these countries and colour them blue.

   b The book suggests that Sierra Leone and Ethiopia are said to be least developed – find these and colour them red.

   c Choose four more countries from map **A** which are most developed – add them to your map, colouring them blue.

   d Choose six more countries from map **B** which are said to be least developed. Add them to your map and colour them red.

2. Write down what you notice about the spread of blue (highly developed countries) and red (least developed countries).

3. Design a double page poster showing the things you think of when 'Development' is mentioned. The left hand side of your poster could show things you think of about more developed countries and the right hand side shows things you think of for less developed countries. 📖

4. Add any new key words from pages 7 to 13 to your word bank.

help!

The following websites can be linked to through www.heinemann.co.uk/hotlinks. They contain information about the countries of the world and could be a useful starting point for your research.

- ✪ United Nations Schools site
- ✪ Social Watch country data
- ✪ Central Intelligence Agency
- ✪ Fact Monster Learning Network

Remember to look for your own useful websites too. (ICT)

Inequalities in development

The statistics used to measure a country's level of development are averages, so they often hide large variations in the real situation of people living there. Table **A** shows the differences in income between the richest 20 per cent and the poorest 20 per cent of the population in five countries.

Country	Poorest 20 per cent	Richest 20 per cent
Brazil	$578	$18 563
Kenya	$238	$4 347
India	$527	$2 641
UK	$3 963	$38 164
USA	$5 800	$51 705

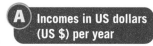
A Incomes in US dollars (US $) per year

Source: UNDP, 1999

Activities

1 **a** Make a copy of table **B**.

   b Calculate how big the difference is between the poorest and richest 20 per cent of the population. Write your answer as a ratio in the last column. The first one has been done for you and the 'How to' box will also help.

Country	Poorest 20 per cent	Richest 20 per cent	Ratio of richest to poorest
Brazil	578	18 563	32 : 1

B

2 Draw a bar graph like **C** to show the figures in the final column of your table.

   a Use the y axis to plot the figures.

   b On the x axis, space out a column for each country.

   c Label each bar with the country name.

3 Describe what your results from activities **1** and **2** show you. For example, which is the most equal country and which has the greatest inequalities? Your work from page 11 might also help you to explain your findings.

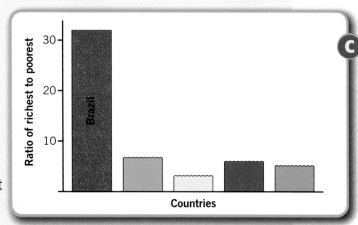
C

How to ...

... calculate ratios

1 To calculate the ratio, divide the larger figure by the smaller figure.

2 The result tells you how many times greater the largest figure is than the smaller figure – the ratio.

3 For example with Brazil:
   $18\,563 \div 578 = 32.11$ so the richest 20 per cent earn 32 times more than the poorest 20 per cent.

4 When writing the ratio, round your result to the nearest whole number, in this example: 32.

Contrasting lifestyles in Kenya

Case Study: Alice

A

My name is Alice and I live here in the West Pokot region of Western Kenya with my husband and four children. I have had seven children in total, but three died before they were even five years old – I was very sad. In our community nearly 150 out of every 1000 children born will die before their fifth birthday. I hope to enrol my children in primary school this year, but it is expensive. My brother has ten children, but only three of them go to primary school. We just don't have enough money – we have just a few goats and our land is not good for farming. Last year we earned just US $120 as a family, even with my husband working at a nearby agricultural project.

Case Study: Christopher

I'm Christopher and I work for a travel company in Nairobi. We take tourists to see our wonderful wildlife and spectacular scenery. It is a good job and last year I earned US $2 640, which is much more than I could earn back in my village. It is still difficult to support my wife and two children, however, especially as she is not working at the moment. She insists on looking after our younger child. So many children die when they are young, but the clinic we go to is very modern and loses only 24 per 1000 before they are five, so we are hopeful. If I keep my job, I will be able to send both my children to primary school, but if we have any more children it could be difficult to educate them all.

B

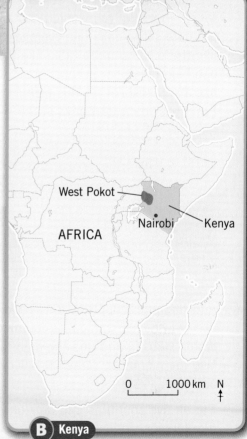

West Pokot

Nairobi

Kenya

AFRICA

0   1000 km   N

B Kenya

Activities

1. Carefully read the case studies of Alice and Christopher. They represent differences in the quality of life in Kenya.

2. Make a copy of the following table and fill in the missing information. The last line has been done for you.

	Alice	Christopher
Income for family		
Under-five mortality for family		
Primary school completion rate for family	30%	100%

3. Using data from both case studies calculate the average level of:

   a income per person (GNP per capita)

   b under-five mortality rate (U5MR)

   c primary school enrolment.

4. The data has been adjusted so that the values you calculate represent the national average for Kenya in 1997. In reality you would need a full data set to calculate averages like these. Copy out a table like the one below with seven rows. You could use a spreadsheet for this task. Enter your data for Kenya in the first row. **ICT**

How to ...

... calculate averages

To calculate the average of several values:

1 Work out the values for each example (in this case, Alice and Christopher).

2 Add these values together.

3 Divide the total by the number of values (in this case two values – one for each case study).

For example, to work out the average GNP per capita:

US $20 (Alice) + US $660 (Christopher) = US $680

US $680 ÷ 2 = US $340

Remember their salaries have to be divided by the number of people in the family. Alice's family earned US $120 but this is shared by six people so it is US $20 each. Christopher's US $2640 is shared by four people.

Country	Average income (GNP per capita)	Under-five mortality rate (per 1000 born)	Primary school enrolment (%)
Kenya			

5. Add the other countries from page 14 into your table, use www.heinemann.co.uk/hotlinks to link to the Social Watch website and find the data for those countries. Use the menus on screen to select your data, countries and year. **ICT**

6. Put all five countries into rank order for each of the development indicators. If you have used a spreadsheet, use the computer to do this. Does the order of countries vary much? **ICT**

C Healthcare is vital for progress in development

Progress in development

In the second half of the twentieth century significant progress was made in world development. For example, life expectancy increased from a global average of 45 years in 1950 to about 67 years at the start of the year 2000. Improvements in health care and higher levels of education have been two of the main developments responsible for this progress. But just as development levels vary between countries and regions, so too does progress in development. Some regions have improved rapidly while other regions show little progress at all. Table **B** shows the progress in development for the world's major regions between 1970 and 1998.

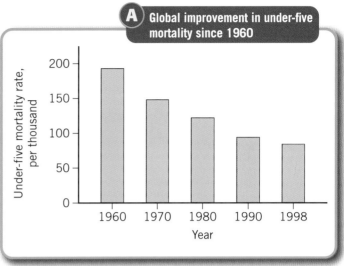

A Global improvement in under-five mortality since 1960

Source: United Nations

Region	Life expectancy (years)		Adult literacy rate (%)		Under-five mortality rate	
	1970	1998	1970	1998	1970	1998
Sub-Saharan Africa	45	49	29	58.5	226	172
Arab States	52	66	31.3	59.7	193	72
East Asia	63	70	81.5	83.4	118	46
South-East Asia	55	66	56.3	88.2	149	57
South Asia	50	63	33.8	54.3	206	106
Latin America and the Caribbean	61	69	72.5	87.7	123	39
Eastern Europe and former USSR	69	69	96.1	98.6	47	33
Industrialised countries	70	76	97	97.4	52	14
World	60	67	n/a	78.8	148	84

B Progress in development between 1970 and 1998

Data taken from UNICEF 1996 and UNDP, 2000

Activities

1 Use figures from table **B** to help in class discussions:
   a Which regions have seen the greatest progress and which the least?
   b Which indicator has shown most progress and which the least?

Case Study
Who decides?

	Percentage involved on regular basis
Men	6
Boys (15–18 years)	11
Boys (under 15 years)	34
Women	94
Girls (15–18 years)	83
Girls (under 15 years)	62

C Water collection as part of daily activities in Kenya

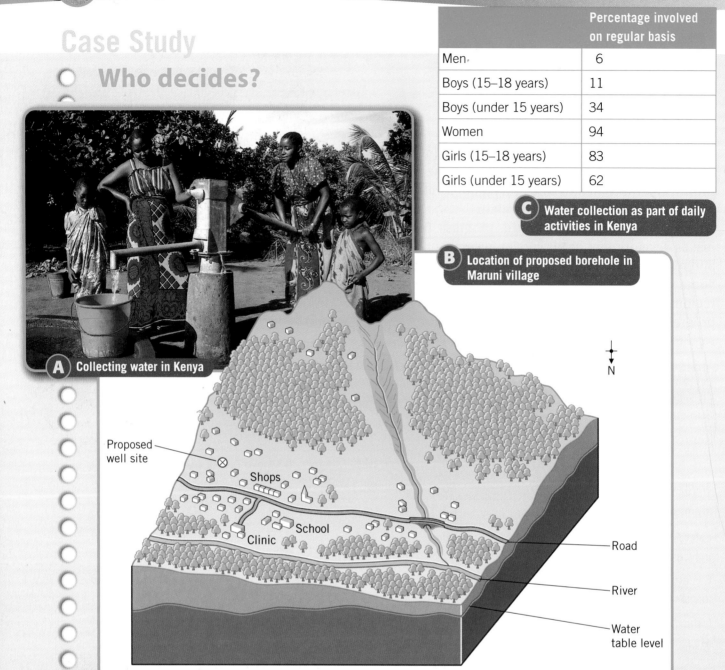

A Collecting water in Kenya

B Location of proposed borehole in Maruni village

Proposed well site

Shops

School

Clinic

N

Road

River

Water table level

Water boost for West Pokot village

Maruni villagers received welcome news today when plans to develop a borehole in their village were announced. Pokot elders finalised plans yesterday with Joseph Lomaria from the regional development authority, who will provide technical assistance, and Philip Saunders, from a UK charity that is funding the project.

Village meetings to discuss water supply problems identified the need for a borehole. At present water is collected from the nearby river, but this is hard work and wastes valuable time. Clean water is found in the rocks under the entire village, but elders decided to drill the borehole in the eastern side of the village where they felt it was most needed.

The local health worker welcomed the announcement. She hopes that a safe water supply would reduce water-related diseases, but stresses the important part played by education in reducing these diseases. She seemed surprised that she had not been consulted on the plans.

The new borehole will be drilled next month and should be in use by the end of the year. There are plans to develop more boreholes if tensions between the Pokot and neighbouring Turkana people subside.

D News extract, 9 October 2000

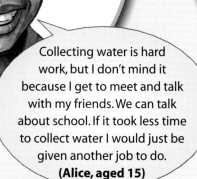

Collecting water is hard work, but I don't mind it because I get to meet and talk with my friends. We can talk about school. If it took less time to collect water I would just be given another job to do.
(Alice, aged 15)

I remember before people lived here when we used to visit with our cattle. When the river was low we would dig holes to get to the water for our cattle, but up here the water holes would dry up in the dry season and we would have to get water from over there, the other side of the village.
(Mzee, old Turkana man from east of village)

I attended the village meetings, but women are not free to speak, we would be told to just keep quiet and let the men make the decisions.
(Perpetua, 34 years old)

I hear what they have said, but do not always agree. When you are young, though, you cannot argue even if you have a better idea.
(Joshua, aged 13)

Activities

1 Suggest three reasons why the project will improve the quality of life for people who live in the district.

2 Say who you think would not be entirely happy with the project and explain why.

3 Do you think that the project should go ahead? Give reasons for your answer.

Sustainable development

B Reforestation in the Sudan, Africa

A Clear-cut forestry (where all the trees are cut down) in British Columbia, Canada

Development does not always bring benefits, especially for the environment. Short-term benefits for some people – jobs and income – often turn into longer-term costs for many people and the environment. For example, the development of the logging and timber industry has led to large-scale deforestation and environmental problems.

Policies to achieve sustainable development have been introduced by many governments and companies. For example, the Forestry Stewardship Council (see **C**) monitor the number of trees being cut down and ensure that an equal number are planted to provide timber for future generations.

Not all development is sustainable, however. Many development projects continue to threaten the environment today and for future generations. For example, using fossil fuels for energy causes problems such as acid rain and releases large quantities of **carbon dioxide (CO_2)** – a greenhouse gas responsible for **global warming**. Fossil fuels are also formed over millions of years, meaning that they cannot be replaced for future generations.

FSC ©

C

Sustainable Development is development that meets the needs of the present without compromising the ability of future generations to meet their own needs.

D From *Our Common Future* World Commission on Environment and Development, 1987

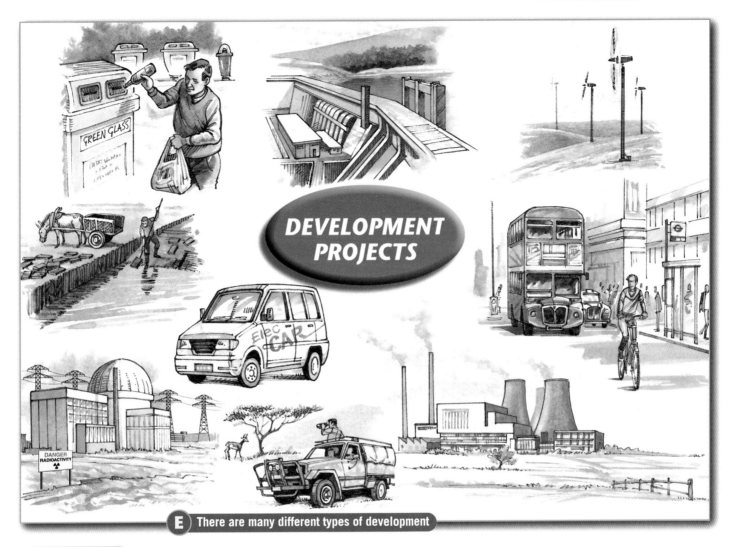

E There are many different types of development

Activities

1. Study the drawings in **E**. Working in a pair or small group, decide which developments you think are sustainable and which are not. Give reasons for your decisions, using evidence to support your argument.

2. Imagine you are responsible for improving sustainable development. Looking at those projects you have listed as unsustainable, what alternatives might you recommend?

3. Create and carry out a research project to investigate how sustainable your school is. To get you started, have a class discussion about:

   - litter
   - use of paper
   - electric lighting / heating
   - use of buildings in holiday periods
   - building materials
   - school dinners.

   a List the sustainable and unsustainable examples that you find.

   b Make a series of recommendations to improve sustainability in your school. Include reasons for your proposed actions and suggest who is responsible for making them work.

Review and reflect

Development into the twenty-first century

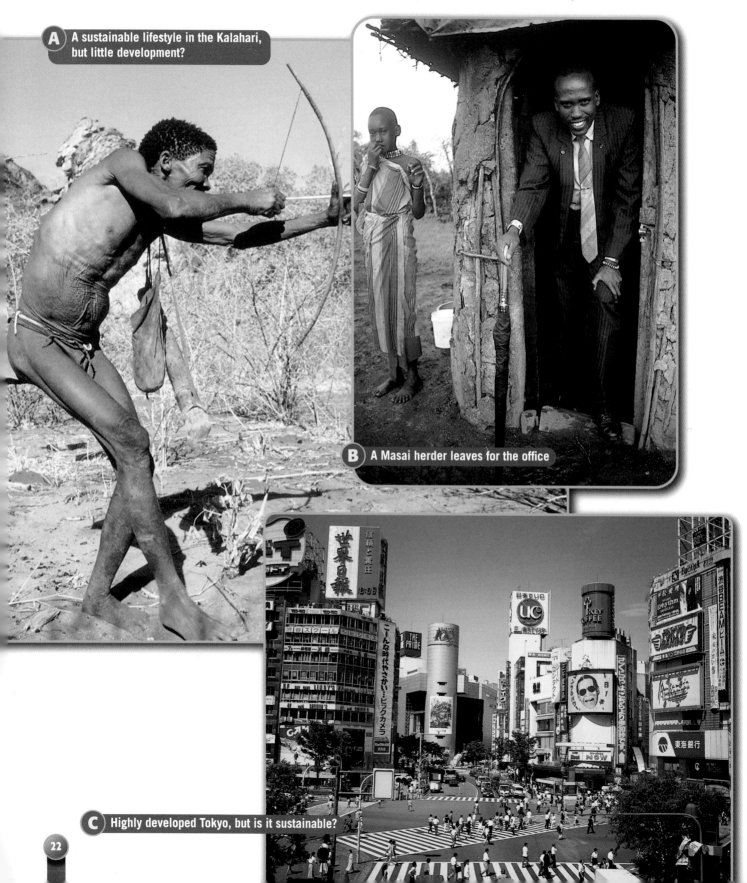

A A sustainable lifestyle in the Kalahari, but little development?

B A Masai herder leaves for the office

C Highly developed Tokyo, but is it sustainable?

As you have learned in this unit, life for most of the world's population improved significantly during the twentieth century. On the whole, people lived longer and were healthier than ever before. However, you have also seen that progress has not been equal and that many people and places still suffer poverty and low standards of living. There are also new concerns about the ability of our planet to support continued progress. People are calling for a rethink about development to make it more sustainable.

Activities

1 Look back at your answers for Activity 2a and check how many of your locations were correct. Were you surprised?

- A The Bronx, New York City, USA
- B Borrowdale 'village' shopping centre, Zimbabwe
- C Schoolchildren in North Vietnam
- D A cybercafé in Dhaka, Bangladesh
- E Forestry, British Columbia
- F Dalian in Liaoning province, NE China
- G Sikh wedding, London
- H Electronics factory, Kuala Lumpur, Malaysia

2 Look back at the photographs in this section. Choose one of the photographs which you think gives the world a great challenge as we move into the twenty-first century.

3 Prepare a speech to explain to your class why you think the photograph poses a great challenge. Divide your talk into:

- I chose photograph ___ .
- I think the great challenge is _____ .
- I think _____ needs to be done.
- This will be difficult because _____ .

Fill in the gaps with words, sentences or a paragraph.

4 Finally, complete your word bank for this unit with new words and terms from pages 14 to 23.

2 France

The changing economic geography of France

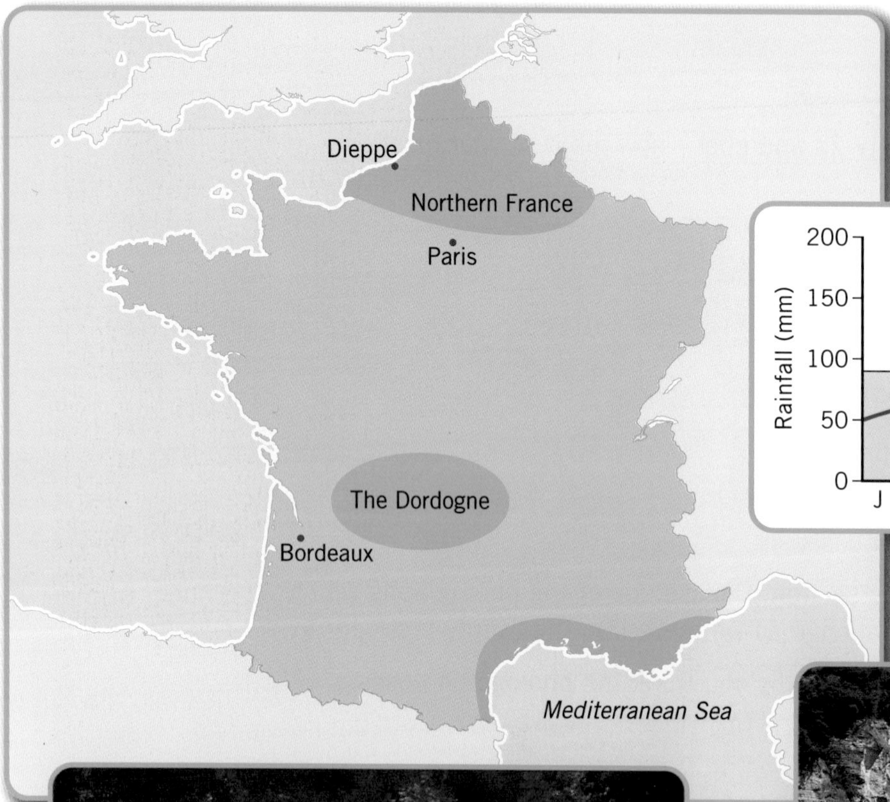
Dieppe
Northern France
Paris
The Dordogne
Bordeaux
Mediterranean Sea

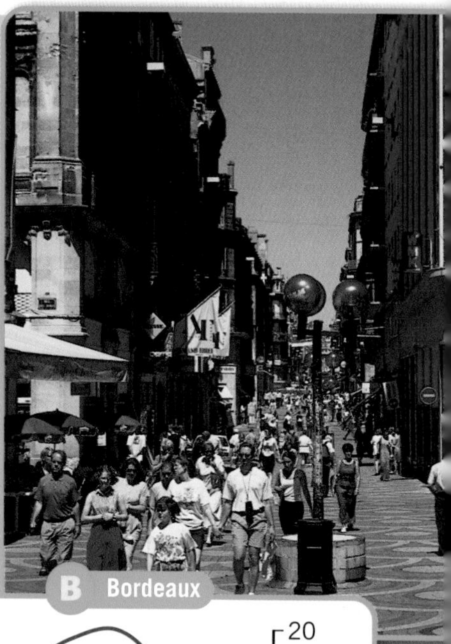

B Bordeaux

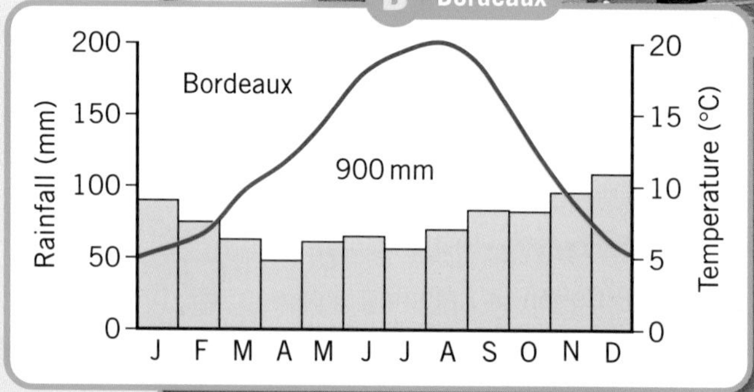
Bordeaux
900 mm
Rainfall (mm)
Temperature (°C)
200
150
100
50
0
20
15
10
5
0
J F M A M J J A S O N D

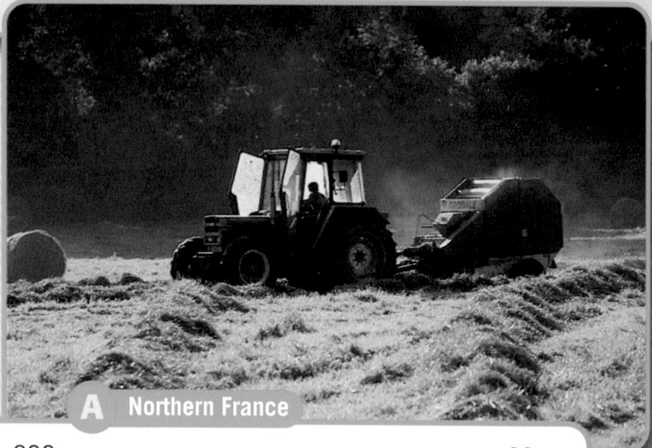

A Northern France

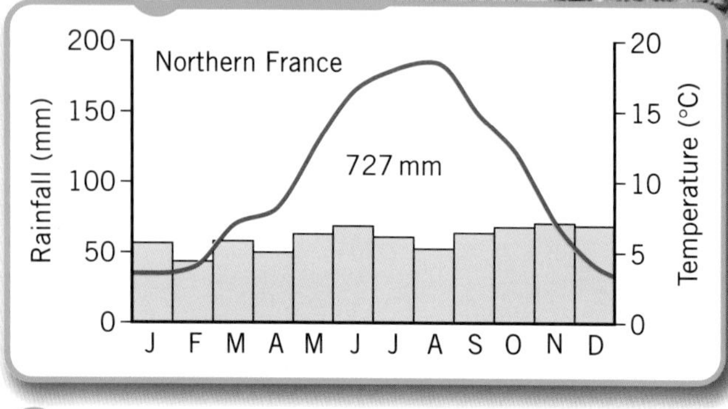
Northern France
727 mm
Rainfall (mm)
Temperature (°C)
200
150
100
50
0
20
15
10
5
0
J F M A M J J A S O N D

C The Dordogne

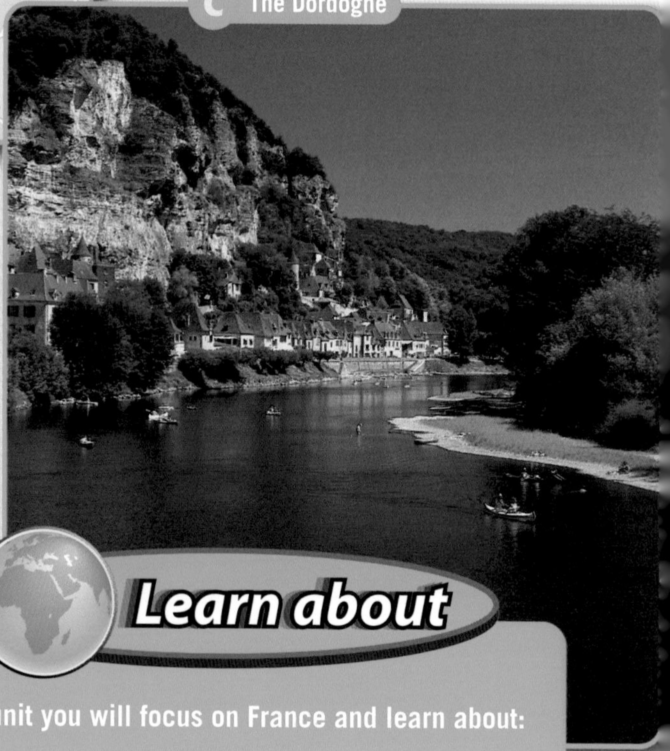

Learn about

In this unit you will focus on France and learn about:

- patterns of economic activity in France
- how economic activities are changing
- the impact of changing economic activities
- the economic links with other countries.

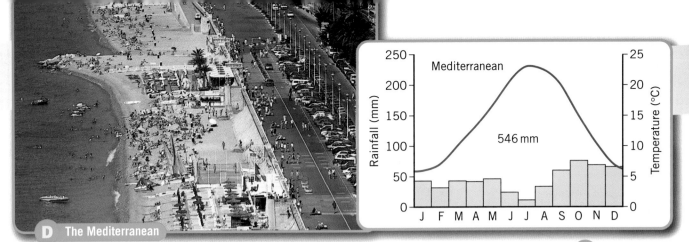

D The Mediterranean

Mediterranean

546 mm

J F M A M J J A S O N D

F Paris

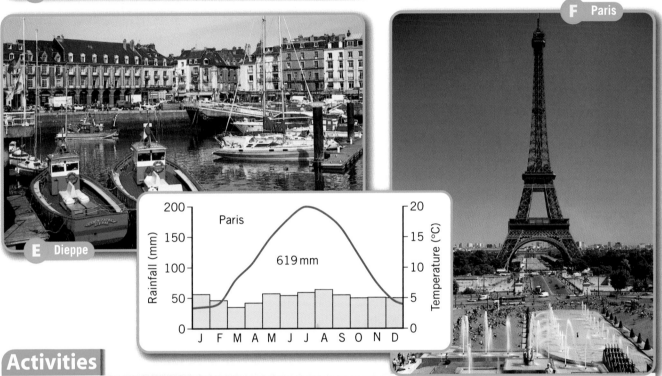

E Dieppe

Paris

619 mm

J F M A M J J A S O N D

Activities

① **a** Study the photographs and climate graphs of France.

b Copy and complete the table below to describe the physical and natural features of France. The first one has been done for you.

	Photo A	Photo B	Photo C
Physical/natural features (e.g. mountains, rivers, trees, hills)	Forest, trees, crops, fields		
Climate (e.g. hot, rainy, sunny)	Sunny, hot, warm		
Economic activity (e.g. farming, industry, services)	Farming, production, machinery/technology, growing		
Settlement (e.g. flats, houses, village, city)	Dispersed, small, little, village		
Population (lots of people, few people, farmers, tourists)	Small, limited, farmers, locals		

② Discuss in class whether you think that economic activities are affected by the natural landscape.

③ Start a word bank of the keywords and terms you have used. 📖

Getting Technical ▼

◎ **Economic activities** are work or activities that people earn money from.

◎ **Primary activities** are activities that extract natural resources from the earth or sea.

◎ **Secondary activities** are activities that make finished or semi-finished goods from raw materials or other partly made products.

◎ **Tertiary activities** are activities that provide a service.

What is France's economy like? How is it changing?

A Harvesting

B Aeronautics industry

C Café in Paris

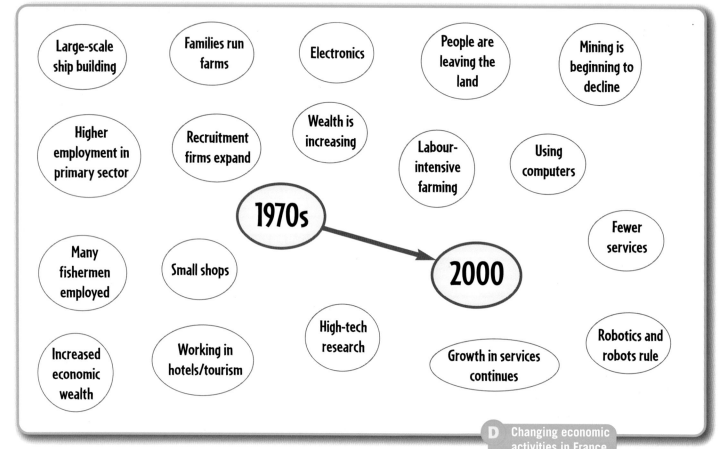

Large-scale ship building

Families run farms

Electronics

People are leaving the land

Mining is beginning to decline

Higher employment in primary sector

Recruitment firms expand

Wealth is increasing

Labour-intensive farming

Using computers

1970s → **2000**

Many fishermen employed

Small shops

Fewer services

Increased economic wealth

Working in hotels/tourism

High-tech research

Growth in services continues

Robotics and robots rule

D Changing economic activities in France

Activities

1. Use the 'Getting Technical' terms on page 25 to help you match the photographs and the words above to primary, secondary or tertiary activities.

2. What changes in the three economic activities do you notice from 1970–2000?

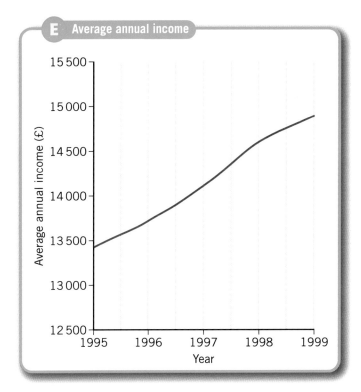

E Average annual income

Average annual income (£) vs Year (1995–1999)

	Oil	Gas	Coal	Electricity	Others
Production	99	35	14	92	11
Consumption	93	34	7	32	9

Figures in million tonnes of oil equivalent (ask your teacher if you do not understand this).

F Energy production and consumption in France, 1999

The number of people out of work in France is high – over 11 per cent of the total working population. The situation is even worse than it appears because:

- many young people stay in education for a long time
- many people are doing their military service.

One reason for unemployment in France is that there are not enough people with the right skills for the jobs available. However, between now and 2010 the number of unemployed people in France will probably fall.

	1995	1996	1997	1998	1999
Number registered unemployed (thousands)	3000	3100	3100	3000	2800
Unemployment rate (%)	11.6	12.3	12.5	11.8	11.2

G Unemployment statistics

Activities

1. Study graph **E**.
   a What was the average income in 1999?
   b What has been the increase in average income between 1995 and 1999?
   c Between which two years was the biggest increase in annual income?
   d Write a sentence to explain the patterns that the graph shows.

2. Use the data in table **F** to draw a bar chart showing the production and consumption of each type of energy. Copy the outline on the right and use different colours to show production and consumption, label the axes and add a title at the top of the chart.

3. In a class discussion, describe what table **G** shows about unemployment in France.

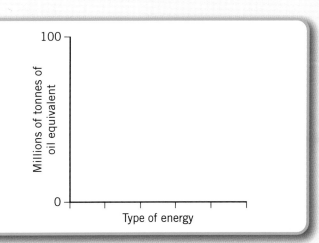

(Bar chart outline: y-axis 0–100 Millions of tonnes of oil equivalent; x-axis Type of energy)

What changes have occurred in the agricultural industry?

Agriculture in France

France has the biggest agricultural industry in Europe. It is the second biggest exporter of agricultural produce in the world behind the USA.

For the past fifty years the number of farmers has been decreasing. In 1970 there were 2.8 million farmers and in 1998 there were just 1.1 million. During the 1990s, 30 000 farmers gave up farming each year.

Despite there being fewer farmers, production has increased. In the 1940s one farmer could produce enough food to feed five people but by 1990 one farmer could produce enough food to feed 30 people.

Production has increased for a number of reasons. There are more machines (tractors have replaced horses) and farmers now use more fertilisers and pesticides.

A An upland farm

France's farming industry has benefited from the support of the European Union. Farmers are given a guaranteed price for their produce as well as grants to help them in many other ways.

However, guaranteed prices meant that farmers were paid money to produce more food, so too much food was produced. This resulted in the 'milk lakes' and 'butter mountains' of the 1980s.

Because of this over-production, support from the European Union is now being reduced. This is causing problems in France because the support favours the most efficient farmers who are often the richest and need the least help.

B Intensive farming

Activities

1 Read the information about farming in France. Choose five phrases from the opposite page about changes in agriculture and use them to complete the sentence below:

Agriculture in France is changing ...

2 a In groups of four, consider the following question. You may use the information on these pages or any knowledge you have about agriculture in France.

Why is the number of farmers in France going down but production is increasing?

b Make a short summary or presentation of your ideas.

Pierre has been adding fertilisers to his crops since 1980.

Jean Claude is guaranteed a set price for all his cows.

Irrigation means that more crops can be grown.

Machinery has made farming a lot quicker.

In 1950 there were 2.3 million farms. In 1990 there were 900 000.

Fabien, my son, lost his job because the farm he worked on bought new machinery.

Guaranteed prices from the European Union have led to over-production.

We use only natural fertilisers on our crops.

There is increasing demand for organically grown food.

Because I use pesticides I lose less of my produce as the bugs that eat the crops are killed.

Seeds and plants are more resistant to diseases now because of genetic engineering.

In 1950 the average farm size was 14 hectares. In 1990 it was 36 hectares.

Advances in technology means that fewer farmers are needed.

In 1950 there were 5.1 million people working in farming compared to 1.1 million in 1998.

Wine makes up a lot of farming exports for France.

The fishing industry is suffering because cheaper fish is being brought in from abroad.

Fewer farmers are needed now because machines are quicker.

Many people have left their farms to work in the city.

Woodland covers a quarter of France. Some timber is exported but even more is imported.

We are the only family-run farm for 10 km.

Selective breeding programmes mean that only the best animals are produced on my farm.

What changes have occurred in the manufacturing industry?

A Grenoble is located in Rhône-Alpes region

Rhône-Alpes

Grenoble

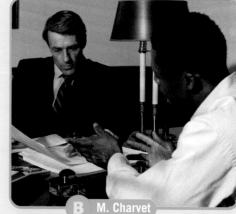

B M. Charvet

Getting Technical ▼

◉ A **technolpole** is an area with new high-tech industries.

C An interview with M. Charvet – the owner of a new factory in a technopole

You: Where and when did you start up your company?

M. Charvet: I built my micro-electronics factory on the technopole in Grenoble, which is in the Rhône-Alpes region, back in 1986.

What did you do before this?

M. Charvet: I previously owned a factory which produced oil-based products.

Why did you change?

M. Charvet: I was affected by a range of issues – my company didn't recover from the oil crisis of 1979.

Why did you choose Grenoble?

M. Charvet: The technopole is a great area to locate – it benefits from being at the centre of networks of motorways, high-speed railways and air routes.

Have other industries followed you?

M. Charvet: You can also find the Nuclear Research Centre, the World Health Organization and the Cancer Research Centre here.

Which areas of France have they left?

M. Charvet: The Lorraine and Nord regions have also suffered from a decline in traditional manufacturing industries.

Tell us about the future.

M. Charvet: The future is bright because the government is actually encouraging technopoles to develop. They give money to improve housing and roads.

D

Old heavy industries have been in decline in the region since the oil

Technopoles were set up in Rhône-Alpes

People who did work in the old industries rarely work in the

Technopoles make good profits so

The government has helped the region by giving

Transport routes are good and provide a link between northern and

The Rhône-Alpes region is France's leading producer of

New high-tech industries locate in areas called

E

technopoles, which are like science parks.

money to improve housing and roads.

region in the 1980s.

southern Europe.

they can pay more for rent and taxes.

new industries because they do not have the skills.

manufactured goods.

crisis of 1979.

Activities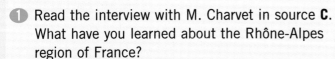

1. Read the interview with M. Charvet in source **C**. What have you learned about the Rhône-Alpes region of France?

2. Study the broken sentences in boxes **D** and **E**. Match the endings of the sentences in **E** with the starts of the sentences in **D**.

What is the pattern of tourism in France?

Tourism is a very important industry in France. This is no surprise when you see what six areas of France can offer the tourist.

Boulogne

Average July temperature: 22 °C

⊙ White cliffs similar to those at Dover run along the coast between Boulogne and Calais.

⊙ Boulogne's historic buildings include the Palais de Justice, the library and the town hall.

⊙ The wide range of restaurants and shops are well worth a visit.

⊙ Will you visit local hypermarkets before you catch the ferry?

Paris

Average July temperature: 24 °C

⊙ The spectacular city of Paris has something to offer everyone: from chic shopping to spectacular shows, Paris has it all.

⊙ Paris is the capital of France and the home of fashion.

⊙ Take a stroll along the Champs-Élysées from the Arc de Triomphe towards the Louvre, where you could see the *Mona Lisa*.

⊙ You might want to visit the Eiffel Tower or the modern art gallery called Musée d'Orsay.

⊙ You could eat in a posh restaurant or enjoy a dinner cruise on the River Seine.

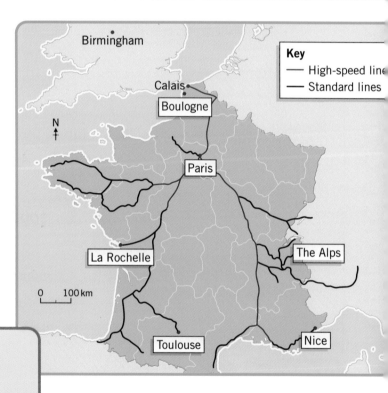

La Rochelle

Average July temperature: 25 °C

⊙ La Rochelle is well known for its historic port.

⊙ The marina is the busiest yachting centre on the French Atlantic.

⊙ Countless cafés and restaurants cluster around the waterfront.

⊙ The cobbled streets of the old town are lined with boutiques.

⊙ The fifteenth-century prison is worth a visit. It has amazing views from the tower.

⊙ You could visit the modern aquarium.

Toulouse

Average July temperature: 25 °C

⊙ The birthplace of Concorde.

⊙ An important industrial and university city.

⊙ You may want to visit Pont Neuf on the River Garonne.

⊙ Tourists are drawn to the two thirteenth-century cathedrals.

⊙ The old town has a lively atmosphere and inexpensive cafés.

⊙ A flea market is held every Sunday.

The Alps

Average July temperature: 28 °C

- Stunning scenery combined with fine hospitality.
- From foothills to dramatic peaks, the Alps are a magnet for visitors in summer and winter.
- Skiers need no introduction to this winter playground.
- You might want to try mountain biking or horse riding in the hills.

Nice

Average July temperature: 28 °C

- The two-kilometre golden beach of Nice has to be seen.
- The promenade is lined with palms and has wonderful views.
- The old town has a blend of balconied buildings, and is home to artists, galleries, shops and, of course, restaurants.
- You could visit the market.
- You could relax in a pavement café and spend your time people-watching!

	Boulogne	La Rochelle	Toulouse	Paris	Alps	Nice
Boulogne		350	700	250	550	800
La Rochelle	350		325	350	550	625
Toulouse	700	325		475	400	375
Paris	250	350	475		350	550
Alps	550	550	400	350		300
Nice	800	625	375	550	300	

A Chart to show distances between possible destinations (km)

Activities

1. Using the information given, select five areas that you would like to visit.

2. If you fly to Paris to start your journey and come home by ferry from Calais, decide your order for visiting the five locations. Use the map of France and the distance chart to help you keep travelling to a minimum.

3. How long will your total journey be?

Case Study

Tourism in Rhône-Alpes

It is estimated that 60 million tourists visit France every year, and some of these will visit the Rhône-Alpes region. The Rhône-Alpes region is partly made up of the Alps, but these are just one of the region's tourist attractions. The region attracts tourists in both summer and winter for a number of reasons.

In the east of the region are the Alps and tourists come to ski and snowboard in the winter and walk in the summer.

Tourists come all year round to visit the River Rhône, where they can enjoy lots of watersports and river walks. The area is also famous for its vineyards.

In the south of the region is the Ardèche Gorge, home to many prehistoric caves. The famous Combe d'Arc cave has drawings that are 20 000 years old.

People also come to the region to visit the major cities. In the cities of Grenoble and Lyons tourists soak up the culture by visiting the museums and art galleries as well as eating in the many restaurants and cafés.

A The River Rhône

Activities

1 Read the information about tourism in Rhône-Alpes.

 a In one colour, identify five things to do and see in Rhône-Alpes.

 b In another colour, identify five facts about tourism in Rhône-Alpes.

2 In groups of three, take the role of one of the following characters each and present/discuss his or her views about tourism in Rhône-Alpes:

 ⑥ tourist (skier)

 ⑥ environmentalist

 ⑥ business person (for example, hotel or shop owner).

The three characters should have a conversation about tourism in Rhône-Alpes. Your conversation should be based around the following points:

 ⑥ whether your character thinks tourism is a good idea

 ⑥ what your character thinks about the effects that tourism has on the environment

 ⑥ your character's opinion about the money tourism brings in to the area.

What energy resources does France have?

France uses many different types of energy. This energy comes from a range of sources.

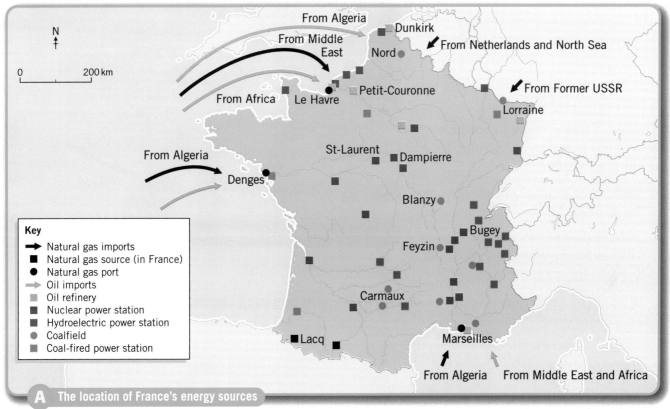

N

0   200 km

From Algeria

From Middle East

From Africa

Dunkirk

From Netherlands and North Sea

Nord

Petit-Couronne

From Former USSR

Le Havre

Lorraine

From Algeria

St-Laurent

Dampierre

Denges

Blanzy

Bugey

Feyzin

Carmaux

Lacq

Marseilles

From Algeria   From Middle East and Africa

Key
➤ Natural gas imports
■ Natural gas source (in France)
● Natural gas port
➤ Oil imports
■ Oil refinery
■ Nuclear power station
■ Hydroelectric power station
● Coalfield
■ Coal-fired power station

A   The location of France's energy sources

Coal

◎ Coal was a very important source of energy in France until recently.

◎ In 1958, 60 million tonnes were produced – 60 per cent of the total energy used in France.

◎ In 1958, 300 000 miners were employed.

◎ By 1989, only 13 million tonnes were produced each year and only 28 000 miners were employed.

◎ The last mine on one of the main coalfields, Nord-Pas-de-Calais, closed in 1991. It was expensive to mine coal there and the type of coal was bad for the miners' health. The environment in this area has been badly affected by spoil tips, derelict mine buildings, and water and air pollution.

B   Coal mining in France

Hydroelectric power (HEP)

C Dam at Tignes, France

- HEP has been welcomed by many people in France as it is a non-polluting source of energy.

- HEP has been developed in the mountains of France where many of the fast-flowing rivers are dammed.

- HEP is a renewable type of energy, so it will never run out.

- The use of water power to produce energy has been slow to develop for a number of reasons:

  - Only small amounts of energy can be produced from each HEP plant.

  - Some people think the plants spoil the landscape where they are built.

  - In the years 1989 to 1990 HEP was badly affected by a shortage of water which greatly reduced output of electricity.

Gas and oil

- Gas and oil are important sources of energy and both are used to generate electricity.

- Gas and oil are both fossil fuels and have two main disadvantages:

  - They are non-renewable (they will run out over time).

  - They cause air pollution.

- Most of the gas and oil used in France is imported from Russia and the Netherlands.

- Since the oil crises in the 1970s, France has cut back on its use of oil.

D Gas pipeline, Manosque

E Drilling for oil

Nuclear power

F   **Nuclear power station at St Alban–St Maurice, on the River Rhône**

- Nuclear power is the main source of France's energy resources.

- In 1974 the French government began to invest in nuclear power stations.

- It takes seven years to build a nuclear reactor, so it was not until the early 1980s that nuclear power could be used.

- There are problems regarding nuclear waste – where should it be stored?

- Nuclear power stations tend to be located near a water source, which is used for cooling.

- Nuclear power has its advantages – it is very efficient and, once the power station has been built, electricity is relatively cheap to make.

- The cost of building nuclear power generators is huge. These costs have led to huge debts for Electricité de France. The state electricity company had a debt of £25.4 billion by 1990.

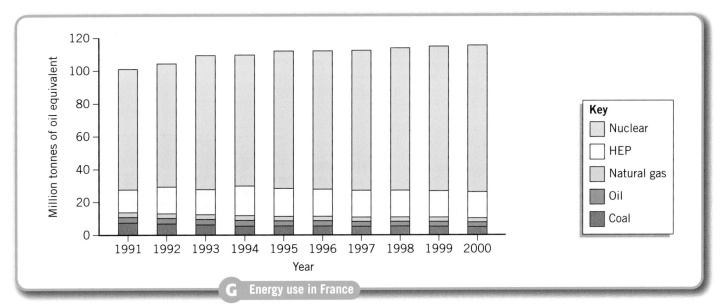

G   **Energy use in France**

Activities

1. Using the information on each type of energy, create a timeline from 1958 to 2001 to show the changes in energy use in France.

2. Copy and complete the table below to show the advantages and disadvantages of each type of energy.

Energy source	Advantages	Disadvantages

3. In a class discussion, find out which kind of energy production is the least popular and which kind is most favoured by your class.

France's energy mix – the nuclear power debate

A The nuclear power station in the Loire valley

B

Nuclear power is now the main source of …

A tidal power station has also been built …

In 1974 the French government began to …

There are lots of problems connected with the problems of nuclear waste because …

Nuclear power stations tend to be located near a water …

Nuclear power uses uranium – the amount needed is small …

HEP has been developed in the mountains …

Recently some people have started to worry about …

C

invest in nuclear power stations.

at Rance in Normandy.

energy in France today.

whether nuclear power is safe.

no one wants it in their neighbourhood.

and the cost is relatively low.

where many of the fast-flowing rivers are dammed.

source, which is used for cooling.

Activities

1 Study the broken sentences in boxes **B** and **C**.

  a Match the starts of the sentences in box **B** with the endings in box **C**.

  b There are two sentences which have nothing to do with nuclear power. Find these 'odd ones out' and write them down in a separate list from the sentences about nuclear power.

2 Read the newspaper article in box **D**. People have a wide range of views about any debate. Some views are based on fact, others on opinion, and some may be a mixture of both.

  a Write down the facts in one colour and the opinions in another colour.

  b Share your facts and opinions with others in your group. How did you decide what was a fact and what was an opinion?

LIFE IN THE SHADOW OF A NUCLEAR POWER STATION

Back in 1952 Madame Goma bought a house in the town of Dampierre. Today, she has a very different neighbour …

I met Madame Goma at her home and we discussed how the energy situation in France had changed over time and how it had affected her life.

During the 1970s the French economy was badly affected by two oil crises. In 1974 the French government decided to build 34 nuclear reactors, followed in 1976 by a further 20. Today nuclear energy represents 75 per cent of the country's electricity production.

I asked Madame Goma what it was like living next to a nuclear power station.

'I feel safe living next to the station because of the very high standard of nuclear safety at the site, and other similar sites in France. I often see officials from the Ministry of Health around the site checking for radioactive releases from the site.'

Madame Goma felt that the site had also had a negative impact upon her life. 'The value of my house has suffered because it is so close to the site, and the continual noise of vehicles in and out of the station is a nuisance.'

Nuclear power has been very successful in France and it seems that it is likely to be so in the future. However, this source of energy is always a controversial issue, having as many disadvantages as advantages.

I doubt that everyone shares the opinions of Madame Goma. I'm sure the nuclear debate will continue for many years to come.

D

Activities

3 Copy the following table and find two things to write in each column. The first one has been started for you.

Madame Goma is happy about nuclear power because …	Madame Goma is unhappy about nuclear power because …
1 'I feel safe…'	**1** 'The value of my house…'
2	**2**

4 Explain to your class how you would feel about a nuclear power station being built near your home. Is your view based on facts or opinions?

International trade

International **trade** is the buying and selling of goods between countries. Goods brought into a country are called **imports** and goods sold to other countries are called **exports**. The difference between the value of imports and the value of exports is called the balance of trade. This may vary from year to year.

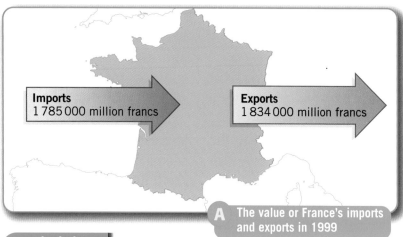

> **Imports**
> 1 785 000 million francs

> **Exports**
> 1 834 000 million francs

A The value or France's imports and exports in 1999

Activities

1. Create a word bank of the key words and terms in the text above – *international trade, imports, exports* and *balance of trade.*

2. Work out France's balance of trade in 1999 by subtracting the value of imports from the value of exports.

3. In 1999 France had a positive balance of trade. Read the first paragraph again, then explain why the balance of trade shows France has a healthy economy.

France's exports

The goods exported from France in 1999 are shown in graph **B**.

		%
Raw materials, metals, chemicals		32
Machines and equipment for industry		25
Consumer goods		14
Cars and trucks		14
Food industry products		9
Farm, forestry and fishing products		4
Energy products		2

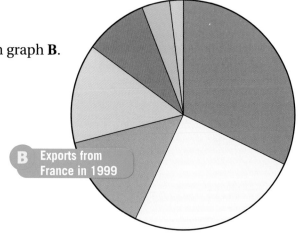

B Exports from France in 1999

France is famous for its exports of food products, clothes and cars. For example, nearly a quarter of cars sold in Europe are French. France's exports of high-tech goods are growing – an example is the aircraft industry, based at Toulouse.

France's imports

		%
Raw materials, metals, chemicals	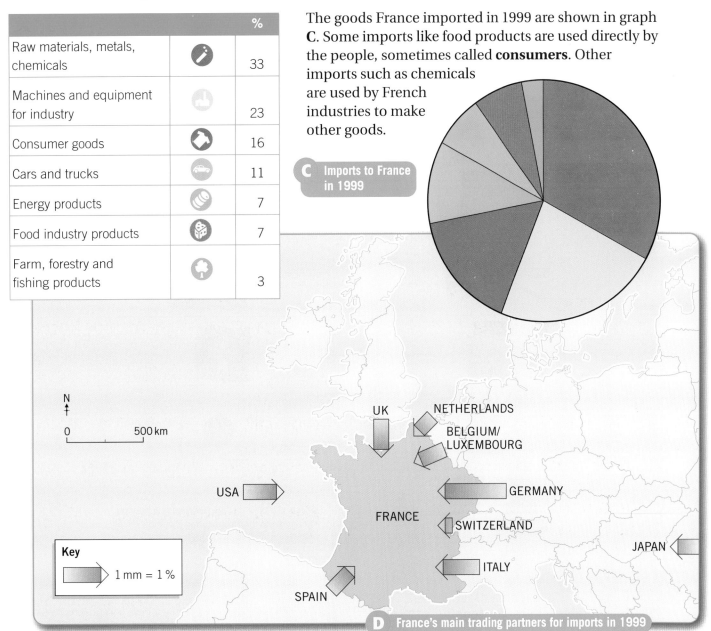	33
Machines and equipment for industry		23
Consumer goods		16
Cars and trucks		11
Energy products		7
Food industry products		7
Farm, forestry and fishing products		3

The goods France imported in 1999 are shown in graph **C**. Some imports like food products are used directly by the people, sometimes called **consumers**. Other imports such as chemicals are used by French industries to make other goods.

C Imports to France in 1999

D France's main trading partners for imports in 1999

Key
1 mm = 1 %

Activities

4 **a** Copy the table below, then use pie graph **C** to work out which imports are for consumers, which are used by industry, or both.

b Work out the total percentage for each category. 123

	Goods	%
Imports for consumers		
Imports for industry		
Imports for consumers and industry		

5 Compare the figures for exports and imports in graphs **B** and **C**. Make three lists of goods:

- Imports to France greater than exports
- Exports from France greater than imports
- Imports to France similar to exports.

6 Study map **D**. Write a short paragraph about the countries where France imports most goods from. You should mention:

- The top three importing countries
- The overall pattern of imports
- Any other interesting points you notice.

France and the European Union

France has economic links with a range of countries. Being part of the European Union means that taxes are not put on goods imported from other EU countries, so these countries form France's major trading partners. France also has trade links with countries that used to be French colonies. Taxes on goods from these countries are usually lower, making them cheaper than goods from other countries.

		% of value			% of value
Germany		16	Belgium/ Luxembourg		8
UK		10	Netherlands		8
Spain		9	Switzerland		4
Italy		9	Japan		2
USA		8			

E France's main trading partners for exports in 1999

Activities

7 Draw a map with proportional arrows showing France's main export partners, using the data in table **B**.

- Set your work out like map **D** on page 41.
- Try using this scale for your arrows: 1mm = 1 per cent of value.

8 Imagine you work for the French Department of Trade and Industry. It is your job to write a report about trade in France. The title of your report is 'France has a good balance of trade'. 📖

help!

Use the following structure for your report:

- You will need an introduction to explain what your report is about. Use the following starters and write clear, short sentences:
  - This is a report about...
  - In this report I will cover...
  - These are the issues to be discussed...
  - As a country we have.

- Write a few paragraphs to state who France trades with and describe the patterns of France's international trade. Think about:
  - Who are France's main trading partners?
  - What are the main imports/exports?
  - What is France's balance of trade like?

- Include values and statistics in your report.

- In your conclusion explain why France has a good balance of trade.

Review and reflect

FRANCE Europe school	**ENERGY** reserves power	**AGRICULTURE** farming land
PARIS London capital city	**TECHNOPOLE** Grenoble science park	**THE ALPS** mountains East
MANUFACTURING industry secondary	**TERTIARY** industry high-tech	
NUCLEAR energy power	**ECONOMY** money country	

Activities

1 In groups of four, read the cards above.

  a Choose one of the cards and describe the word in capitals to the other members of your group *without using any of the other words on the card.*

  b Choose another card and draw a picture to represent the word in capitals.

  c Design some other cards to try out in your group.

2 Add key words and terms you have used to your word bank. You could start with the words on the cards above.

The global fashion industry

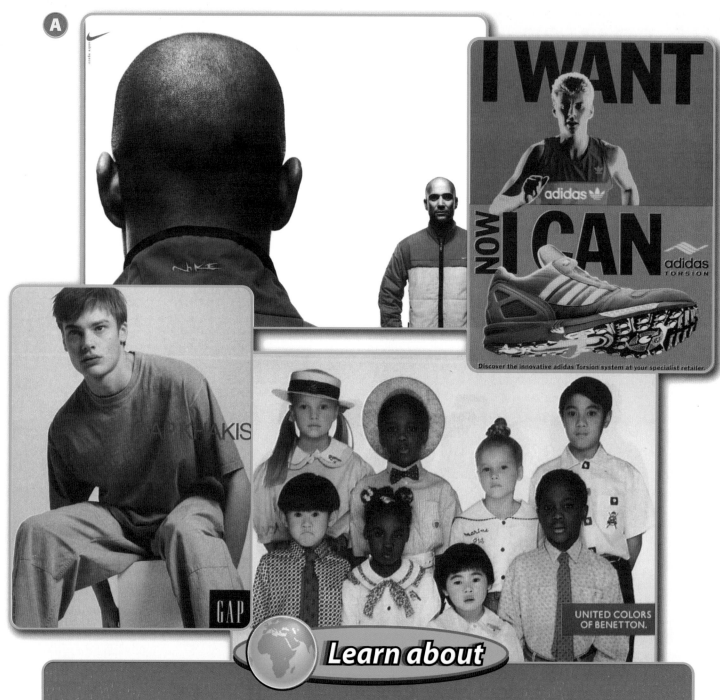

A

Learn about

The fashion industry has an impact on people all around the world. It is said to be a *global* industry. The industry links people who live in less developed countries (LEDCs) with people who live in more developed countries (MEDCs). In this unit you will learn:

- what the global fashion industry is like
- how people, places and environments are connected
- what is meant by *globalisation*
- who takes part in the chain of production and what happens if the chain is broken
- what the future of global fashion might be like.

B A sweatshop in Cambodia

C Catwalk shows help sell fashions

D Some views of global fashion

I don't think workers in the fashion industry are badly treated. Their wages may be low, but it's better than having no job.

I like to wear fashionable clothes like the trendy pop stars or sports people. I'm more interested in what the clothes look like than where they come from.

I think clothing workers like us have a right to decent working conditions and pay. I sewed on collars for £4.64 a month. I often worked overtime, without pay. I worked from 7am to 10pm, or sometimes all night.

Powerful advertising forces young people to keep up with their friends by buying expensive brand names.

I don't see why I should buy clothes that create such inequalities for the world's workers. I would rather help to make working conditions fairer.

Activities

1 Look at the adverts in **A** and have a class discussion about these questions:

- Who are the adverts aimed at?
- How do the adverts persuade people to buy the goods?
- What *don't* the adverts tell you?

2 Look at photos **B** and **C**. How do they show that the fashion industry is a global industry?

3 Look at the views about global fashion in **D**. Put the quotes into two lists:

- Those which support the global industry.
- Those which are concerned about some things to do with the industry.

4 What is your opinion about the industry?

5 Start your word bank of terms for this unit, using the glossary on pages 142–143 to find meanings. Display the key terms as a wall display about global fashion in your classroom. 📖

Who's the fashion victim?

The fashion industry connects people all around the world. After all, we all wear clothes!

Think about these questions

- Where do your clothes come from?
- What sort of lives do people who make your clothes live?
- How do the clothes get to you from the place where they are made?
- How does the money you pay get divided up?

Did you know?

- The fashion industry has been an economic activity for hundreds of years.
- Today, new materials such as rayon and polyester are used alongside cotton and wool.
- The industry makes huge profits.

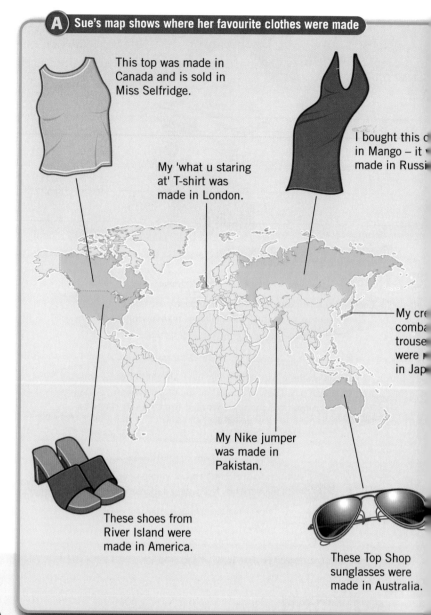

A Sue's map shows where her favourite clothes were made

This top was made in Canada and is sold in Miss Selfridge.

I bought this d in Mango – it made in Russi

My 'what u staring at' T-shirt was made in London.

My cre comba trouse were in Jap

My Nike jumper was made in Pakistan.

These shoes from River Island were made in America.

These Top Shop sunglasses were made in Australia.

Activities

1. Look at the labels on your clothes (include your trainers / shoes).
   a. Find the *brand name* (the company name).
   b. Use a search engine on the Internet to find the headquarters. (ICT)
   c. Make a copy of the table and fill in the first two columns.

Company / Brand name	Where is the headquarters?	Where is the item of clothing made?

2. Fill in the third column.
3. Share some of the results with your friends and add their information to your table.
4. a. Ask your teacher for a large, blank map of the world. Together with your teacher, mark the map in blue where the headquarters are and mark in red where the clothes are made.
   b. Discuss in class any patterns that can be seen, then write up your findings.

Fashion companies will try to make their products for the cheapest price and with the least trouble. Many companies locate production all over the world, often in poorer countries where the minimum wage is lower. As the needs of a company and the conditions in countries change, the company may move production somewhere else.

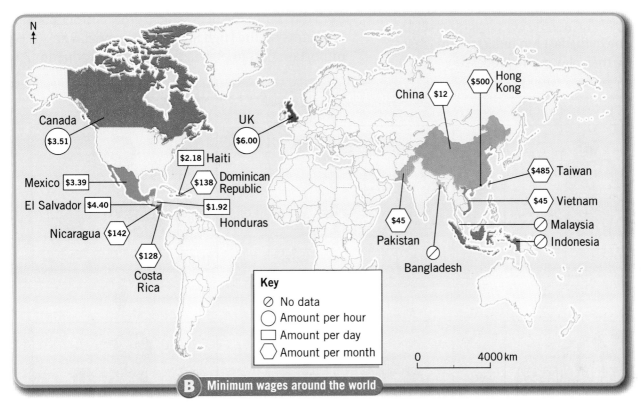

N

Canada
$3.51

UK
$6.00

$2.18 Haiti

Mexico $3.39
$138 Dominican Republic

El Salvador $4.40
$1.92

Nicaragua $142
Honduras

$128
Costa Rica

China $12

$500 Hong Kong

$485 Taiwan

$45 Vietnam

Malaysia
Indonesia

$45
Pakistan

Bangladesh

Key
⊘ No data
◯ Amount per hour
▢ Amount per day
⬡ Amount per month

0   4000 km

B Minimum wages around the world

Activities ①②③

⑤ Map **B** shows minimum wage data for selected countries around the world.

a First, calculate the *minimum wage per month* for the countries which have data per day or per hour. Use a 40-hour week as a guide.

b List all the places in rank order and draw a graph to show the results. Write about your graph – what do the results show?

c Use an atlas or the Internet to find out the GNP (Gross National Product) and the HDI (Human Development Index) for two of the countries on map **B** and four of the countries on the map you did for activity **4**. The maps on page 12 may also help you.

d In class, discuss the title of this section 'Who's the fashion victim?'

Global fashion links

Countries everywhere are **interdependent** – they rely upon other places for trade to keep their economies going. Some places have been linked together for many years, while others are relatively new **trading partners**. Who are the key players around the globe in the fashion industry and what parts do they play in the process?

The fashion industry – chains of production

The fashion industry involves millions of people each day. From the people who grow cotton to shop assistants on the High Street, everyone has an important part to play in the chain of production.

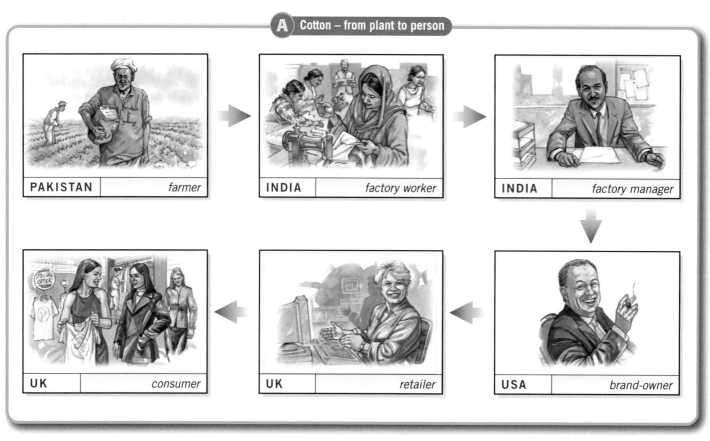

A Cotton – from plant to person

PAKISTAN — *farmer*

INDIA — *factory worker*

INDIA — *factory manager*

UK — *consumer*

UK — *retailer*

USA — *brand-owner*

Activities

1. Drawing **A** shows the chain of production for a T-shirt. Plot the people and their locations on a world map, connecting them with arrows. Plot yourself as the consumer (customer) at the end of the chain. Discuss these questions as a group:
   - How many places are connected?
   - Who has power in the chain? Explain what you think.
   - Are there winners and losers? If so, who?

2. The people in different parts of the production chain are shown in **B**. Divide your class into six groups that take on one role each. Discuss the answers to these questions in your group, then feed back to the class:
   - Who is this person?
   - Who do they work for?
   - How are they linked in the chain?
   - What is their life like?
   - Who makes their decisions?

B

Farmer

- The farmer works seven days a week to produce the cotton for the factories.
- The farmer must grow good quality cotton. Any spare money is put back into the land, so the farmer is often in debt.
- In a good year the profit made from selling the crop is good, but when the weather is poor the farmer's family may go hungry.

Manufacturer

- The manufacturer produces goods for the brand-owner.
- To stay in business, he must charge the brand-owner as little as possible.
- Low profits mean little money to improve factory conditions.
- There are problems with health and safety in the factory.

Retailer

- The retailer sells the product to the public and takes a large share of the price – about £23 from a £50 garment.
- The retailer buys goods from the brand-owners at the lowest possible price to increase profits.
- The retailer likes to buy 'brand named' goods because they can be sold for higher prices.

Consumer

- The consumer buys the product from the retailer in the high street.
- The consumer wants to pay a low price for the product, but will pay more for quality goods with a brand name.
- The consumer is concerned about poor conditions in factories in LEDCs.

Factory worker

- The factory worker works for twelve hours a day, six days a week. The factory is cramped, dark and dusty, and workers are often badly treated.
- The pay is only 60p an hour, hardly enough to live on, but jobs in the city are hard to find.
- The work is very tiring and there is no time off for illness. Pregnant women are sacked.

Brand-owner

- The brand-owner wants to be the world market leader to make as much money as possible.
- To keep costs down and stay in business they locate in countries that pay low wages for factory work.
- The brand-owner tries to protect the factory workers from poor working conditions.
- The brand-owner will pay famous people large amounts of money to help sell their product.
- The company has an annual turnover of £2.4bn and makes a profit of £190 million.

Activities

3. If the people in the chain are all involved in the production of a garment which costs US $100, decide as a group how much each person *should* get as their share.

   Make sure that you can justify your reasons.

4. Why do you think your ideas from activity **3** are unlikely to happen?

The information on these two pages looks at the people at the start of the production process – the factory workers. Many garments and shoes are made in *developing countries* (LEDCs). Here labour is cheaper and factory costs are lower, so the brand-owners can make bigger profits.

Life in these factories has been well publicised in the media and many have been called **'sweatshops'**. For example, in 2000 a documentary in the BBC *Panorama* series exposed factories who were producing goods for Gap and Nike, and challenged some of the working practices in Cambodia.

Adidas attacked for Asian 'sweatshops'

C Adapted from an article by Andrew Osborn, *The Guardian*, 23 November 2000

Sportswear giant Adidas was named in the European parliament yesterday as a company that pays poverty wages and forces its workforce to do overtime. British MP Richard Howitt introduced an Indonesian speaker who said that the company did not follow its own code of conduct, which was supposed to protect factory workers.

In the Tuntex factory in Jakarta, 1700 workers, mostly women, make jackets and socks. 'They get less than a dollar a day and have to work long hours', said Rainy Hutarabat, a local community mission worker.

Gap and Nike: No sweat?

Panorama reveals that Gap and Nike have been using a factory in Cambodia that breaks their own strict codes of conduct and anti-sweatshop rules.

The two hugely successful international brands claim that regular checking makes sure that most factories are safe places to work. However, the *Panorama* team uncovered sweatshop working conditions and child labour at the June Textiles factory in Cambodia.

Sun Thyda, 12, lied about her age to get the job. She says: 'I didn't want to come here, but we're very poor so I had to come.'

Six other girls spoke about their working conditions. All work seven days a week, often up to 16 hours a day.

Nike and Gap told *Panorama* that they are working with the factory to improve conditions. Nike may even stop using the factory altogether in December.

E Adapted from the BBC *Panorama* website, 15 October 2000

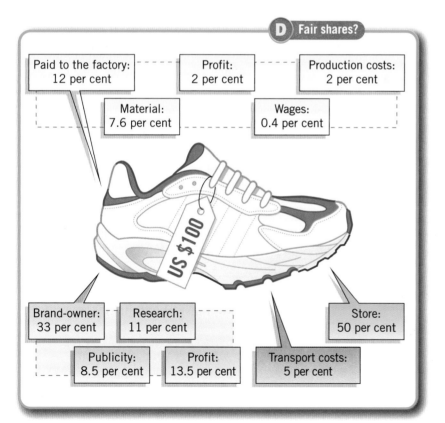

D Fair shares?

Paid to the factory: 12 per cent

Profit: 2 per cent

Production costs: 2 per cent

Material: 7.6 per cent

Wages: 0.4 per cent

US $100

Brand-owner: 33 per cent

Research: 11 per cent

Store: 50 per cent

Publicity: 8.5 per cent

Profit: 13.5 per cent

Transport costs: 5 per cent

F

My job

What is your job?
I make clothing for American companies.

Where do you work?
In a factory in Tehuacàn, Mexico.

How many hours do you work each week?
We all work from 8 am to 7 pm, Monday to Friday. If any work is rejected, we may stay until 10 pm. On Saturdays we work from 8 am to 2 pm, but we often don't leave until 4 pm. We don't get breaks, not even to eat.

How much money do you earn?
US $28 a week.

What do you pay for with your salary?
Food, housing, clothes, transport and other essentials.

Do you ever have money left over?
No. The government says that enough food for my family costs about US $70 a week. That's without housing and the other things we have to buy.

Do you get benefits?   No.

Can you get promotion?   No.

Do you work at the weekend?
Yes, always Saturday, sometimes Sunday.

Where do you eat lunch?   On the street.

What kind of relationship do you have with your boss?   He yells at me and shoves me.

What happens if you arrive late for work?
They take 10 pesos from our pay if we're five minutes late. Sometimes they won't let us into the factory until 9 am – they take away 30 pesos for that.

Are you paid if you work overtime?   No.

How much holiday do you get?
We can take off a week at Christmas, but we have to make it up by working on Sundays.

Can you join a union?   No

Are you punished for staying home if you are sick?   Yes.

Do people who do a dangerous job get protective equipment?   No.

How many times can you go to the toilet at work each day?   The supervisor gets mad if we go more than once.

Activities

1. Look at the information on these two pages, then do some research to find out more about working conditions in parts of the developing world. You can find useful website links at www.heinemann.co.uk/hotlinks

   Present your findings as a poster; think of a catchy headline and use a desktop publishing program for a really professional finish. ICT 📖

2. Look at the questionnaire in **F**. Ask a relative or friend who is in work to answer the same questions, then compare your findings with **F** and present them to the class. Produce a display to compare UK jobs with those in developing countries.

3. Check that you have all the words in bold type in your word bank. Add them to the class display if you have one. 📖

What happens when the chain of production is broken?

Case Study: Kukdong factory, Mexico

In January 2001 the 800 workers at the Kukdong factory in Atlixco, Mexico went on strike to protest at the working conditions in their factory. Kukdong International is a Korean-based producer with branches in Indonesia, Brazil and Mexico. The factory produces goods for Nike, Reebok and many US universities.

The strike began on Tuesday January 9 – read how the story unfolded, as reported on the Internet by the Clean Clothes Campaign and by Nike using the links at www.heinemann.co.uk/hotlinks.

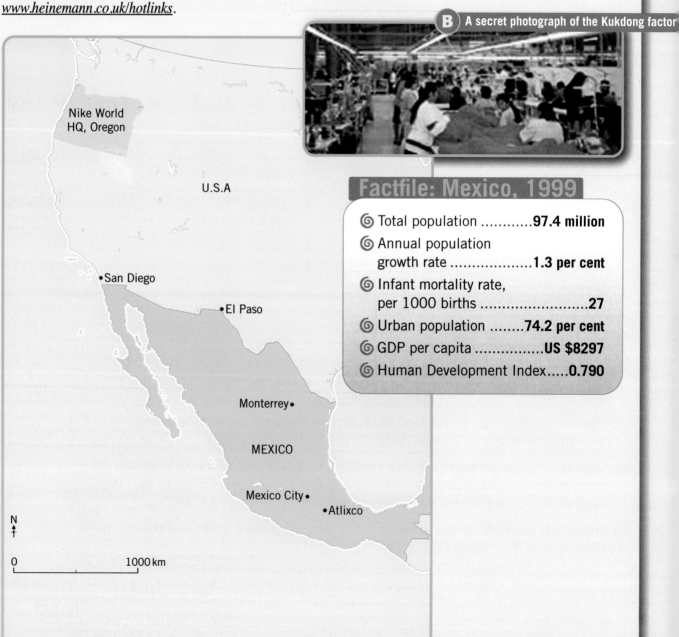

B A secret photograph of the Kukdong factory

Nike World HQ, Oregon

U.S.A

San Diego

El Paso

Factfile: Mexico, 1999

- ⑥ Total population ....**97.4 million**
- ⑥ Annual population growth rate ....**1.3 per cent**
- ⑥ Infant mortality rate, per 1000 births **27**
- ⑥ Urban population ....**74.2 per cent**
- ⑥ GDP per capita ....**US $8297**
- ⑥ Human Development Index.....**0.790**

Monterrey•

MEXICO

Mexico City•

•Atlixco

N

0   1000 km

January 9 2001

All 800 workers go on strike to protest at unjust sackings and other abuses of workers' rights in the factory.

The workers demand that:

1 All workers return to work, including the sacked workers.
2 The company agrees not to fire or punish anyone for taking part in the strike.
3 The company recognises the Kukdong Workers' Coalition as the Union for the workers and agrees to talk with them.

The workers plan to continue the strike until the company meets their demands. Police in full riot gear attack 300 workers who were guarding the factory gates.

January 16 2001

The company agrees to allow the workers to come back to work without anyone being punished.

January 17 2001

The workers try to return to work but they are locked out and told that they are fired.

January 19 2001

The clothing companies and the factory management agree that the factory should be inspected. An independent company, Verite, was chosen, which was accredited by the Fair Labour Association (FLA). It was asked to write a report both to the FLA and to the companies involved.

'Our first task was to bring calm to the factory. We employed an independent factory inspector to make sure that the rights of 500 returning workers were respected.'

Adapted from the words of Dusty Kidd, Vice-President for corporate responsibility, Nike

February 5 2001

The inspectors begin their five-day visit. They use the same standards as in many other countries throughout the world.

March 13 2001

More than 500 of the 800 workers return to work. Nike, Reebok and Kukdong management are working closely with local government officials and aid workers to help workers return to their jobs at Kukdong without reprisals. They help the factory management to make changes, based on the inspectors' report. The improvement plan and Verite's report can be found at Nike's website through www.heinemann.co.uk/hotlinks

March 18 2001

The Kukdong workers meet to form an independent trade union.

March 27 2001

Reports from Mexico say that the atmosphere in the Kukdong plant is calmer than it has been in months. The leaders of the independent union are investigating workers' grievances and meeting with management on their behalf.

The next step is the legal recognition of the union in Mexico, which should allow fairer working practices in the Kukdong factory in Atlixco.

'Nike is committed to taking action to ensure that Kukdong provides a fair, safe and healthy environment for the men and women working there. Nike will also continue to hold Kukdong to the standards outlined in Nike's Code of Conduct to strengthen our commitment to long-term improvement for workers making Nike products around the world.'

Dusty Kidd, Vice-President for corporate responsibility, Nike

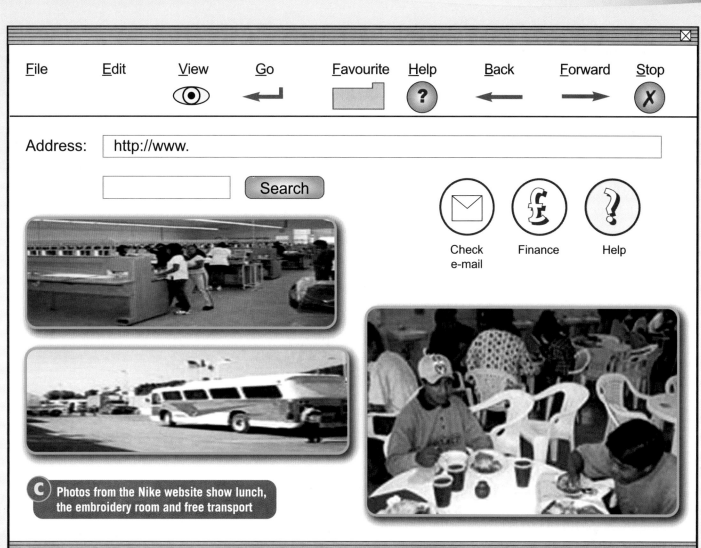

File   Edit   View   Go   Favourite   Help   Back   Forward   Stop

Address: http://www.

Search

Check e-mail   Finance   Help

C Photos from the Nike website show lunch, the embroidery room and free transport

Activities

1. Read about the strike at the Kukdong Factory. Take the role of the workers, the factory-owners and Nike in turn and summarise the cause of the strike from their point of view in no more than 20 words for each.

2. Discuss the issues raised by the strike and make some comments under these headings to include in a debate about fair working practices in factories:

   - Factory workers' rights
   - Factory-owner's opinion
   - Role of the brand-owners (Nike, Reebok, etc.).

3. Consider the effect that the strike had on the people in each part of the chain of production. Using the groups that you were in for activity **2** on page 48, discuss the impact on you and then share your ideas by taping an interview or writing a report for a newspaper about the strike.

4. Think of other ways that the chain of production might be broken. Make a list of these ways and write down how you think that each problem could be overcome. Set it out as a table like the one below.

Problem	Solution

Globalisation – what is it and what drives it?

Everyone in the world is becoming more and more connected together. Many of the clothes and shoes you wear were made by people thousands of miles away. Jobs in the UK, as well as in the countries where these clothes are produced, depend upon trade with faraway places. People travel more, money flows around the world with the push of a button, and the World Wide Web makes it easier than ever before to connect and keep in touch. This process is called *globalisation*.

As you saw in Unit 1, the UK government has promised to make globalisation work for everyone. They have set targets for international development for completion by 2015.

Globalisation has been speeded up by large companies who can afford to locate all over the world, usually searching for bigger markets and higher profits. They are called **transnational corporations** (TNCs) and include Ford, Coca Cola, General Motors, Shell, IBM, Unilever, Sony and Nestlé. Major TNCs in the fashion industry include sportswear giants like Nike, Reebok and Adidas, and companies such as Gap, Levi Strauss and H&M. These brand names are recognised the world over and their logos are among the most widely recognised images on the planet. The annual incomes of the leading ten TNCs are shown in table **A**. For comparison, the annual incomes (GDP) of ten selected countries are shown in **B**.

> '*The world is SMALLER than it has ever been. Its six billion citizens are CLOSER to each other than ever before in history*'
>
> **UK Department for International Development (DFID), 2000**

A Annual income of the ten largest TNCs (billions of US dollars)

Corporation	Annual income	Nationality
Exxon Mobil	232.75	USA
Walmart	191.33	USA
General Motors	178.76	USA
Ford Motor Company	170.06	USA
Daimler Chrysler	152.11	Germany, USA
Royal Dutch Shell	149.15	Netherlands, UK
BP	148.06	UK
General Electric	129.85	USA
Toyota Motor Company	112.94	Japan
Mitsubishi	110.33	Japan

Data for 2000 from **Fortune** *website*

B GDP of ten selected countries (billions of US dollars)

Country	GDP
Bangladesh	46.0
Chile	67.5
Indonesia	142.5
Ireland	93.4
Israel	100.8
Norway	152.9
Portugal	113.7
Saudia Arabia	139.4
Singapore	84.9
Switzerland	258.6

Data for 1999 from **UNDP** *website*

Supporters of globalisation argue that TNCs bring jobs and new technology to the developing nations of the world. Those against globalisation say they have become too powerful and that they control the global economy. Some TNCs are wealthier and more powerful than many countries. Of the world's richest 100 economies, 49 are countries and 51 are TNCs.

Activities

1. Look at tables **A** and **B**, which show the amount of money made by some corporations and countries. Draw a new table which merges the data from both tables into rank order, from the highest to the lowest.
The table could be presented like this.

Corporation (TNC) or Country	Income / GDP (billions of US $)	Rank
Exxon Mobil	232.75	1
Switzerland	193.9	2

Shade the companies red and the countries blue. The first two have been done for you.

2. Describe what your new table shows, looking carefully at the nearest neighbour to each TNC in terms of wealth.

3. Plot the countries shown in table **B** and TNC headquarters on to a world map to show their locations. Describe what the map shows. Is there a 'power base' from the data you have been given? Look for the most powerful places in the world. Does the data surprise you?

Natural
• Which resources does it use (local/distant)?
• What are the impacts on the environment (local/regional/global/elsewhere)?

Who decides?
• Where are the decision-makers located?
• Who has control over the process?
• What is the impact on/of local/national democratic processes?

Where is the company located:
• HQ?
• branch plants?

Economic
• What are the positive/negative economic effects (local/national/elsewhere)?
• Who gains? Who loses?
• Where are these located?

Social
• What are the cultural impacts?
• Who gains? Who loses?
• What is the social impact?
• Where are the winners and losers located in society?

C The Development Compass Rose

© DEC, Birmingham

Fair trade in fashion?

The fashion industry is a global economic activity with complicated links between people who may be thousands of miles apart. It is a difficult task to make sure that working conditions are the same the world over. Many transnational companies have Codes of Conduct and ways to check that production of clothing is safe and fair.

During the 1970s and 1980s, more and more TNCs used subcontractors (other companies) to produce their goods. A well known example is Nike. They employ 5000 people directly, but a further 600 000 workers are employed by smaller companies who produce clothes and shoes for Nike.

The International Labour Organisation, which is part of the United Nations, has written international labour standards. Companies like Nike use these to draw up Codes of Conduct for their factories.

Activities

1. In pairs, discuss what you think should be included in a Code of Conduct for workers in factories producing clothing or shoes. Look at the 'My job' questionnaire on page 51 to help you think about the working conditions in some factories. Present this as a poster which could be displayed in the workplace.

2. Compare your code of conduct with one that you have researched from the Internet. Choose a well known company and use a search engine like Lycos, Yahoo! or Google to search for the information. Start with a general search for the clothing company, then use their website to find their Code of Conduct. ICT

3. Design a fair trade T-shirt which highlights the issues in global fashion today.

Review and reflect

What is the future for fashion?

In an increasingly globalised world, where people and places are connected more closely than ever before, what does the future hold? People will always need clothes, but how will the production of those items change and develop? Will trade unions and demands for workers' rights be a powerful force, or will the transnational companies continue to lead the world and have a major say in what happens in factories in less developed countries?

Activities

1. Read through all the work you have completed, then look through Unit 3 again.
   Look back at your opinion about fashion from question **4** on page 45, and decide whether your opinion on global fashion has changed. Think about:

   - the winners and losers in the process
   - who benefits from the fashion trade
   - how people and places are connected.

   Write down twenty words which you think of after working on this unit. Ask a friend to pick five of your words and explain to them what you think of when the word is mentioned.

2. Complete a crystal ball exercise. Look into the future, twenty years from now.
   What might the fashion industry be like then, and why? You might like to think about what you *expect* to happen and what you *want* to happen. Write up and explain your predictions to the class.

4 Tourism – good or bad?

What is tourism?

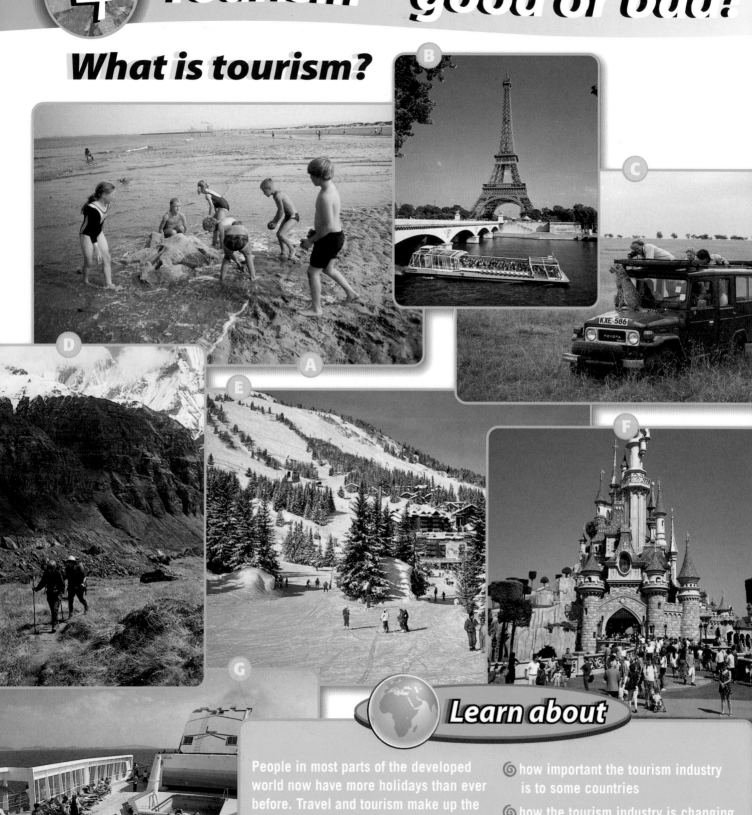

Learn about

People in most parts of the developed world now have more holidays than ever before. Travel and tourism make up the world's largest group of industries. In this unit you will learn:

⑥ the different types of holidays people can take

⑥ what jobs are provided by the tourism industry

⑥ how important the tourism industry is to some countries

⑥ how the tourism industry is changing

⑥ how the impact of visitors on the places they visit can be positive or negative

⑥ how tourism can be more sustainable.

How important is tourism as an economic activity?

Fact file: Tourism

- ⊚ Tourism employs more people than any other industry in the world.
- ⊚ Income from international tourism was US $476 billion in 2000.
- ⊚ More tourists (75.5 million) visited France than any other country in 2000.
- ⊚ The USA received US $85.2 billion from tourism in 2000 – more than any other country.

Activities

1 a With a partner, look at photographs **A** to **G** and make a list of all the different types of holiday they show and as many others as you can think of.

   b How many different groups or headings can you fit those types of holiday in to?

2 a For each photograph, make a list of all the attractions of that area.

   b Identify whether these attractions are physical/natural (e.g. snow in photograph **D**), or human (e.g. the Eiffel Tower in photograph **B**).

3 Choose one photograph of a place you would like to visit. Can you think of any negative impacts people might have on the area in the photograph you have chosen?

4 Choose either photograph **A** or photograph **D**. Imagine you are going to take a holiday in Margate or the Alps. Make a list of all the jobs that will be created by that holiday from the moment you see it advertised on the TV. Decide which type of industry each job belongs to. 'Getting Technical' on page 25 of this book will help. The list has been started for you (below).

Primary sector jobs	Secondary sector jobs	Tertiary sector jobs
Farmers to supply food to hotels	Construction worker at hotel	Travel agent

5 Shade all the jobs which you think will be seasonal, i.e. only available at certain times of the year. Explain why this is the case.

6 Copy and complete a large version of the Venn diagram on the right by writing each job in the correct section.

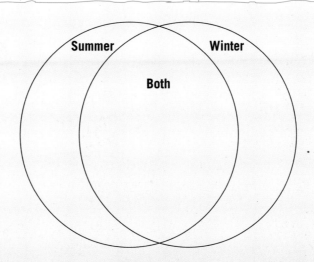

Summer   Winter

Both

How and why is the tourism industry changing?

Tourism is a constantly changing industry. Many things affect where people choose to go on holiday. For example, some people like to go to familiar places, others are looking for somewhere different. There are also fashions for different types of holidays and, of course, for most people price is important. Many holiday resorts have gone through a period of growth followed by a period of decline as people change their choice of holiday. The graphs and tables on these pages show some of the changing patterns of holidays taken by people from the UK and some reasons for those patterns.

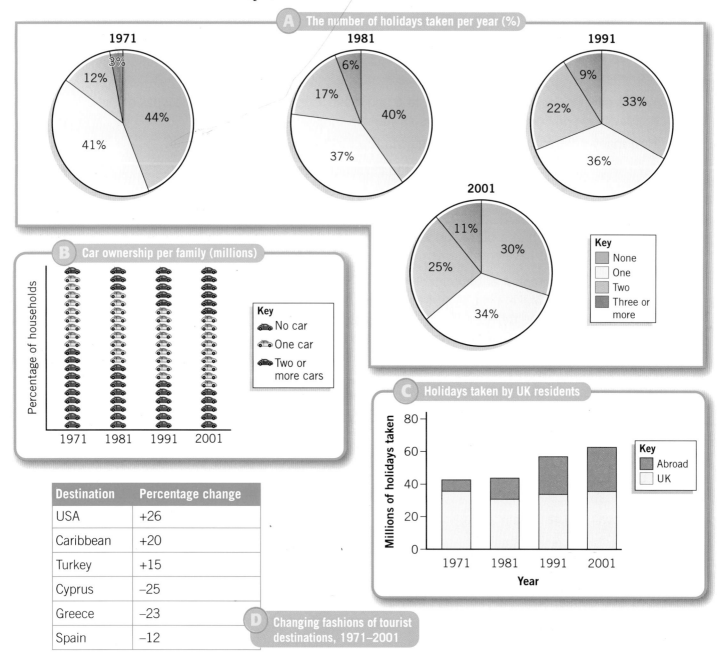

A The number of holidays taken per year (%)

1971
3%
12%
44%
41%

1981
6%
17%
40%
37%

1991
9%
33%
22%
36%

2001
11%
30%
25%
34%

Key
None
One
Two
Three or more

B Car ownership per family (millions)

Percentage of households
1971 1981 1991 2001

Key
No car
One car
Two or more cars

C Holidays taken by UK residents

Millions of holidays taken
80
60
40
20
0
1971 1981 1991 2001
Year

Key
Abroad
UK

Destination	Percentage change
USA	+26
Caribbean	+20
Turkey	+15
Cyprus	−25
Greece	−23
Spain	−12

D Changing fashions of tourist destinations, 1971–2001

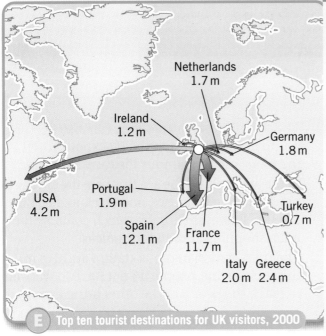

Netherlands
1.7 m

Ireland
1.2 m

Germany
1.8 m

USA
4.2 m

Portugal
1.9 m

Turkey
0.7 m

Spain
12.1 m

France
11.7 m

Italy Greece
2.0 m 2.4 m

E Top ten tourist destinations for UK visitors, 2000

Blackpool to Benidorm

- On the first Saturday of July 1945, trains carried a record 102 890 trippers to Blackpool. Beaches had been off-limits since the start of the Second World War.

- The Holiday with Pay Act turned this weekend trip into a two-week annual adventure for workers.

- The working class went to Blackpool or Margate. The middle classes chose the more select beaches of Bournemouth and Eastbourne.

- In the summer of 1948 there were almost 8000 cases of polio in Britain. Many were blamed on the polluted beaches around Britain's coast.

- In 1948 one in 20 British holidaymakers went to a Butlin's holiday camp for their holidays.

- By the 1960s millions of Britons began going on holiday to the Mediterranean Sea and in 1970 5.7 million British people chose to go to Spain on holiday, mostly through package tours.

- By 2000, 40 per cent of all holidays taken by Britons were spent abroad.

F Adapted from *The Guardian*, July 1999

Activities

1 Copy and complete the following paragraphs:

Since 1971 the number of holidays taken by people who live in Great Britain has increased from _____ million to _____ million. An increasing number of these have been taken abroad and by 2001 _____ per cent of holidays taken were outside Great Britain.

Reasons for the increase in holidays might include the fact that more people own cars. In 1971 ____ million families had no car, but by 2001 this figure had decreased to _____ million. The increase in the number of motorways has also made holiday areas more accessible.

In 1971, 56 per cent of the population took at least one holiday. By 2001 this had risen to _____ per cent. This is because _____ .

The introduction of the package holiday meant that it was easy to travel abroad and in 2000 the three most popular holiday destinations for Britons were _____ , _____ and _____ .

2 Prepare a report for the British Tourist Authority on the main changes and trends in the tourism industry in the UK since 1971. Include sections on:

- the total demand for holidays
- the types of holidays people choose to go on
- the destinations of the holidaymakers.

a Begin each section of the report with an enquiry question. For example, the first paragraph could start with: 'How has the demand for holidays changed and what are the reasons for this?'

b Include in your report graphs, diagrams, maps and pictures.

3 **Extension**

You may wish to make a database and generate your graphs using a computer. Lots more information is available from tourism websites (see www.heinemann.co.uk/hotlinks for suggestions). **ICT**

Case Study

What is the impact of the tourist industry in Blackpool and St Lucia?

Blackpool

Blackpool is a typical British seaside resort. The coming of the railway in 1846 made Blackpool a busy, popular holiday destination as it was within an hour's ride of the cotton towns of Manchester, Bolton and Rochdale. For many of the mill workers, the highlight of the year was the outing to Blackpool. With the arrival of cars and coaches, Blackpool continued to grow and today 16 million people visit the town each year.

- There are 11 km of wide sandy beach backed by a promenade where people like to walk and take the sea air.
- Lining the promenade are the more expensive hotels where guests are willing to pay more to overlook the sea.

- The major tourist attractions can also be found in this zone, such as Blackpool Tower, the piers and the famous Pleasure Beach.
- In the area behind the sea front are the cheaper hotels and guest houses, and Blackpool's CBD (Central Business District), which contains the main shopping area and the offices.
- The train station and bus station are also in this area so that people do not have to walk far to reach the beach or the other attractions.

A

The Illuminations ......

First put up in 1879, the lights stretch for about nine kilometres along the sea front. They attract 8 million visitors a year and shine for 66 nights, extending the season by nine weeks at a time when most other resorts have closed down.

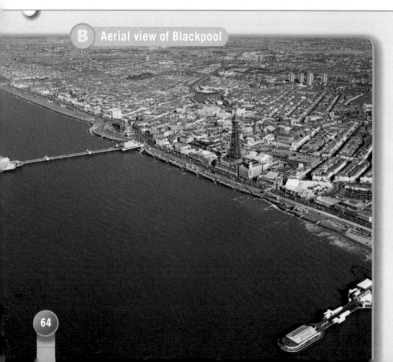
B Aerial view of Blackpool

Blackpool is no longer the most popular place for family holidays. The number of visitors staying and spending money in Blackpool has fallen in the past 30 years as people go abroad for the better weather. People are not only changing their holiday destinations, they are also changing the types of holidays they take. Far more holidaymakers camp, climb, visit rainforests and theme parks, or travel long distances than ever before.

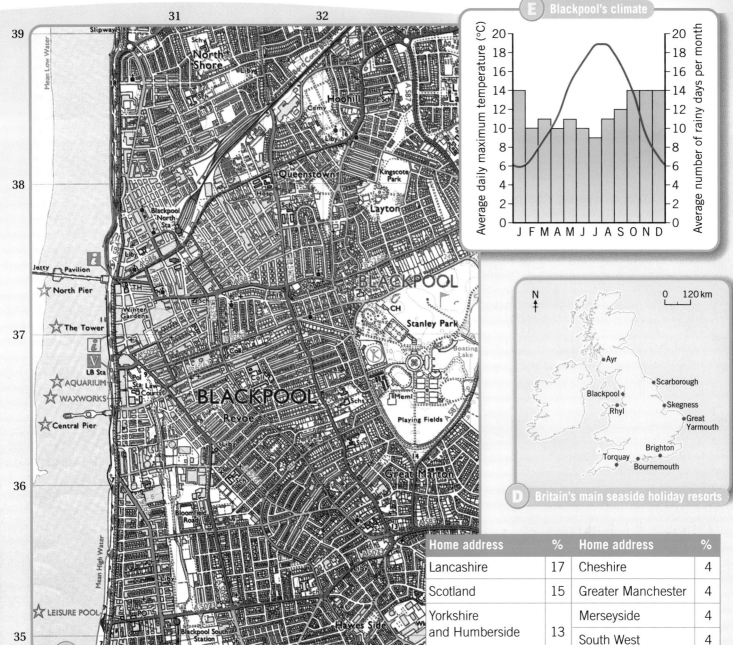

E Blackpool's climate

D Britain's main seaside holiday resorts

F Extract from an OS map of Blackpool, scale 1 : 25 000

Home address	%	Home address	%
Lancashire	17	Cheshire	4
Scotland	15	Greater Manchester	4
Yorkshire and Humberside	13	Merseyside	4
		South West	4
West Midlands	9	East Midlands	3
Wales	6	Greater London	3
South East	6	Derbyshire	3
North East	6	Other	3

G Home addresses of visitors to Blackpool, July 2000

Activities

1. Write a paragraph to explain why Blackpool has declined as a popular destination for holidaymakers.

2. Make a list of all the ways that Blackpool tries to extend its season to provide more work.

3. **a** Draw a sketch map of Blackpool from map **F**. Label on Blackpool's tourist attractions. The symbols on the map, and photographs **A** and **B** will help you.

   b Underline your labels for Blackpool's natural attractions in green, and the human attractions in red.

4. Look at the figures in table **G** and also at map **D**. In a class discussion, work out why certain areas of Britain send more people to Blackpool than others.

help!

Think about climate, attractions and alternative destinations.

St Lucia

A St Lucia, a tropical paradise

St Lucia is an island of 616 km² in the Windward Islands chain, 160 km west of Barbados. The capital city of Castries and the surrounding villages in the north are home to 40 per cent of the island's population and these are also the most popular tourist areas.

Until recently the main income for the islanders has been growing and exporting bananas. Today, however, the island receives as much income from tourism as it does from the bananas. Although the St Lucians realise the importance of tourism to their country, they are working hard to avoid ruining their land with overbuilding. The island is also growing a wider range of foods such as mangoes, tomatoes, limes and oranges. These are sold to the hotels. The need to import food has been reduced.

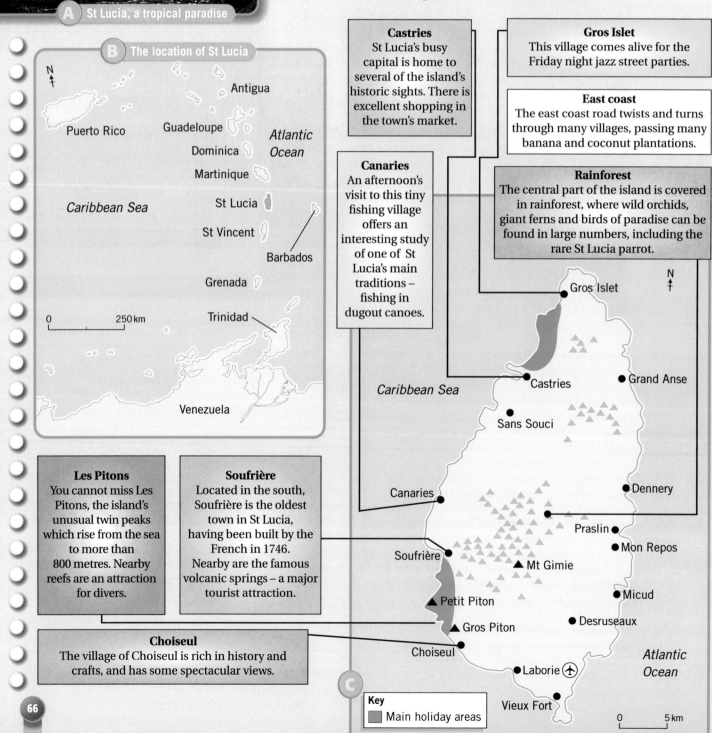

B The location of St Lucia

Castries
St Lucia's busy capital is home to several of the island's historic sights. There is excellent shopping in the town's market.

Gros Islet
This village comes alive for the Friday night jazz street parties.

East coast
The east coast road twists and turns through many villages, passing many banana and coconut plantations.

Canaries
An afternoon's visit to this tiny fishing village offers an interesting study of one of St Lucia's main traditions – fishing in dugout canoes.

Rainforest
The central part of the island is covered in rainforest, where wild orchids, giant ferns and birds of paradise can be found in large numbers, including the rare St Lucia parrot.

Les Pitons
You cannot miss Les Pitons, the island's unusual twin peaks which rise from the sea to more than 800 metres. Nearby reefs are an attraction for divers.

Soufrière
Located in the south, Soufrière is the oldest town in St Lucia, having been built by the French in 1746. Nearby are the famous volcanic springs – a major tourist attraction.

Choiseul
The village of Choiseul is rich in history and crafts, and has some spectacular views.

Key
Main holiday areas

❤ *Weddings and honeymoons in St Lucia*

St Lucia, known for its lush tropical beauty and breathtaking scenery, is highly regarded as a romantic treat and a honeymoon and wedding destination. Most of the hotels in St Lucia provide special facilities for couples getting married on the island; some will also provide a private room or suite for the ceremony, if you prefer.

D

ST LUCIA MIRROR
WATER SHORTAGE

Some hotel owners are unhappy with the local water supply. Berthia Parle, owner of the Bay Gardens Hotel, said that water was sometimes rationed. She added that the local water company cannot cope with demand, even though they have recently increased charges.

Mrs Parle also went on to explain that hotels in the north of the island had water shortages. A new pump had been promised but was not yet installed.

E Adapted from a newspaper article

Month	Average number of rainy days per month	Average maximum daily temperature (°C)
January	18	28
February	13	28
March	13	29
April	10	31
May	16	31
June	21	31
July	23	31
August	22	31
September	21	31
October	19	31
November	20	29
December	19	28

F St Lucia's climate

BRITISH FOREIGN OFFICE ADVICE TO VISITORS

Last Updated: 11 May 2001
Most visits to St Lucia are trouble-free, but visitors should be aware that crime is on the increase and muggings can occur at any time, day or night. Visitors should not become complacent because of the friendly, laid-back nature of the island.

G Advice to visitors

H Arrivals of tourists to St Lucia in 1999

Numbers of tourists (thousands)

Americas: 158 800
Europe: 98 555
Other: 3 228

Origin/region

Activities

1. Draw a sketch map of St Lucia and label it with the attractions of the island for a holidaymaker. Use one colour to label the natural attractions (for example, Les Pitons) and another colour to label the human attractions (for example, the market at Castries).

2. Use table **F** to draw a climate graph for St Lucia. **123**

3. Write a five-minute script for a television holiday programme which compares Blackpool and St Lucia. Use the following headings:

   ⑥ What is the resort like?

   ⑥ What does it offer visitors? (Think about natural and human attractions.)

   ⑥ Who goes there and where are they from?

   ⑥ How and why does the resort benefit or suffer from the tourism industry? (Say which are social, economic or environmental effects.)

How can tourism be more sustainable?

Many developing countries are becoming popular tourist destinations. Tourism can bring many benefits, such as jobs. It can also result in costs, such as pollution or environmental damage.

People in these countries are also made more aware of the inequalities between themselves and the visitors in terms of their quality of life. Visitors can sometimes offend the local people by the way they dress or the lack of respect they show for local customs and religion.

The key is to strike a balance so that holidaymakers can enjoy themselves without destroying what attracted them in the first place. This type of tourism is known as **sustainable tourism**.

Sustainable tourism also means making sure that local people benefit from the industry, not just big tour companies. For example, local people need to be involved in making decisions which affect their lives. Tourists who arrive in places like St Lucia can play their part in sustainable tourism. They can become **ecotourists**.

A Adapted from an extract in *Holiday Which?*, Spring 1999

How to be an ecotourist

Before you go
- Get rid of unnecessary packaging and swap plastic for paper.
- Try to take eco-friendly shampoos and sun lotions.

While you're away
- Get out and be adventurous – if you always stay in the hotel, little money will get through to local people.
- Try local dishes and drinks instead of eating food which has been imported.

In the hotel
- Don't waste energy. Turn off the lights and air-conditioning when you leave your room.
- Don't waste water.

Out and about
- Consider using public transport or hire a bicycle to get around.
- Buy presents and souvenirs from local craftspeople and pay a fair price.
- Ask permission before photographing people.
- Dress appropriately – don't offend local people. Remember you are a guest in their country.

Activities

1. Write a sentence to explain what is meant by sustainable tourism.

2. Copy and complete the table to show how five suggestions in box **A** encourage sustainable tourism. One has been done for you.

Suggestion	Reason(s)
Get rid of unnecessary packaging	Host country does not have to burn or bury additional waste

Review and reflect

What are the effects of tourism?

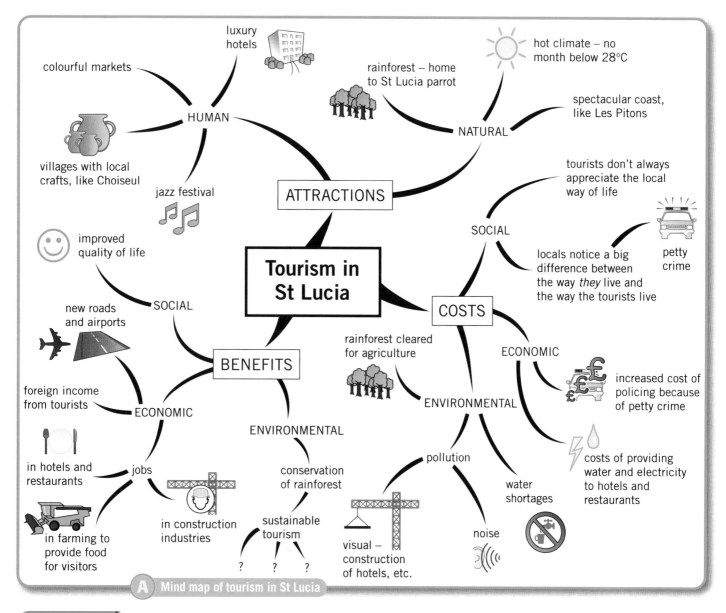

A Mind map of tourism in St Lucia

Activities

1 **a** Look carefully at the mind map above. It shows information about the tourism industry in St Lucia – an economically less developed country. Use the ideas in it to draw a similar mind map for a holiday resort in the United Kingdom, or another more economically developed country of your choice for example in France or Spain.

    b Collect some holiday brochures and use information from pages 61 to 68 here to help investigate them. If you are able to, add facts from research you have carried out on the Internet. **ICT**

2 Add the key words from this unit to your word bank. 📖

5 Comparing countries

What do we do when we compare countries?

Comparing two or more countries means studying the two countries side by side to see how far they are similar and how far they are different. By comparing two countries we will end up with a much better understanding of both countries.

日本

B Japan

中国

A China, the Middle Kingdom

C

D

Learn about

What is it really like to live in another country? Why is every country different? Why do parts of some countries seem very familiar? Finding out about different places is an important geographical skill. In this unit you will learn:

- about two countries in different states of economic development – China and Japan
- how and why China and Japan are geographically similar
- how and why China and Japan are geographically different
- why places such as China and Japan change
- how countries such as China and Japan are linked together
- how to locate places and environments.

Activities

1. Before you begin finding out about another country, you need to think about what you already know or do not know about that country.

   a Make two lists, one for China and one for Japan. Write down in each list anything you already know about each country (e.g. main cities, the names of large companies, sports personalities, famous people, events).

   b Share your lists with a partner. How do they compare?

   c Write down five questions that you would like to ask to find out more about China and Japan.

2. Look at photographs **C–H**. Make a large copy of the table below and fill in the empty cells. The information for photograph **C** has been done for you.

   a For the photographs that show people, decide what the people are doing (for example working, travelling, shopping, on holiday).

   b For each photograph, study the landscape. Is it, for example, flat, mountainous, countryside, built up, urban?

   c Which photographs do you think were taken in China and which were taken in Japan? Give a reason for your choice. (The actual locations of the photographs are given on page 92 – but don't cheat!)

Photo	The people	The landscape	China or Japan	My reason
C	Tourists are visiting a famous place.	It's countryside and it's hilly.	China	The Great Wall is a famous tourist place.
D				

Where are China and Japan?

The first step of any geographical enquiry is to ask questions. Often the first question you need to ask is 'where are the places located?' You need a variety of maps, atlases and globes to answer this question fully.

You can start by simply saying that both China and Japan are in Asia. A more accurate way is to use lines of latitude and longitude.

Using map **A** we can see that China is between 20°N and 55°N (lines of latitude) and between 75°E and 135°E (lines of longitude).

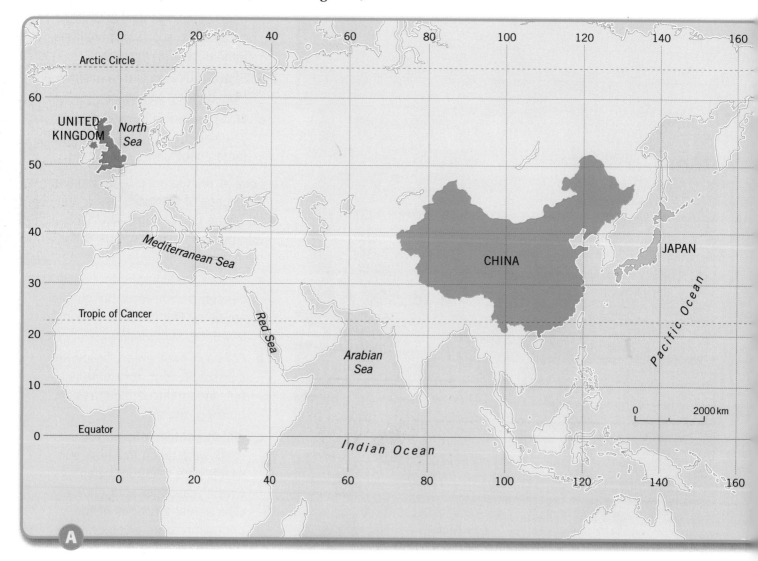

A

Country	Land area (km²)
UK	244 880
China	9 596 960
Japan	377 800

B How much land?

Activities

1. Use map **A** to locate Japan using lines of latitude and longitude.

2. Working with your teacher, estimate the central point of China and work out the latitude and longitude of this point. Do the same for Japan.

3. Work out the location of the UK using latitude and longitude.

Country	Average population density (people per km²)	Total population (millions of people)
UK	237	59
China	126	1259
Japan	332	126

C How many people?

D An image of Japan from a satellite – an island nation made from nearly 4000 different islands

E A world image from a satellite – China is a country large enough to be home to nearly a quarter of the world's population

help!

✪ Remember that we are comparing these countries. How much bigger is China than Japan? How much larger is the population of China than Japan? Include this information in your summary.

Activities

4. Study satellite images **D** and **E**. With the help of your atlas, make a list of the oceans and seas that surround the islands of Japan.

5. Make a list of the countries that have a border with China.

6. Make a copy of the table below. Write a short summary to fill in the empty cells. Two answers have been done for you.

	China	Japan
Size of country	A huge country, nearly 40 times bigger bigger than the UK.	
Population		
Location		A group of islands in the Pacific Ocean.

China – where do people live and work?

1 056 666	a month
243 846	a week
34 835	a day
1 451	an hour
24	a minute

A The increase in the Chinese population, 1996

To continue with your geographical enquiry, you need to decide what data to use. On this page, you will find lots of data about the population of China.

○ How many people live there?

○ Is the population increasing?

○ Is the population spread out or clustered?

○ How many people live in cities / the countryside?

○ What sorts of work do people do?

B Urbanisation – a high density of people

Key
Population density
National average per sq km: 126

	Eastern region 383
	Central region 147
	Western region 51

C China's population density

D Rural areas – a low density of people

When the People's Republic of China was declared in 1949, there was virtually no agricultural or industrial development.

Fact file

The People's Republic of China

- China has changed a great deal in the last 50 years.
- People used to have a life expectancy of just 32 years. Now, people can expect to live until they are 70.
- Agriculture and industry have made great advances. Today, China (including Hong Kong) is the fourth largest trading nation in the world.

F A wide range of products are made in China

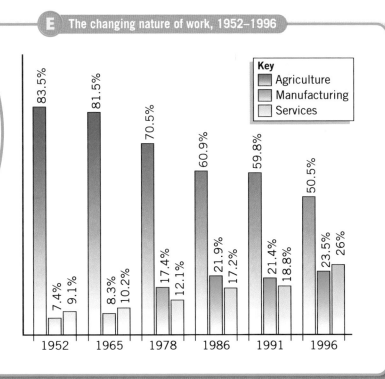

E The changing nature of work, 1952–1996

Key
- Agriculture
- Manufacturing
- Services

1952: 83.5%, 7.4%, 9.1%
1965: 81.5%, 8.3%, 10.2%
1978: 70.5%, 17.4%, 12.1%
1986: 60.9%, 21.9%, 17.2%
1991: 59.8%, 21.4%, 18.8%
1996: 50.5%, 23.5%, 26%

Activities

1 Study map **C**.

  a Some parts of China have very few people. Write down the names of these areas.

  b Some parts of China have very many people. Write down the names of these areas.

  c Look at where the main towns and cities are located. By 2025 it is expected that more people will live in cities than in rural areas. How will this change where people live in China?

2 Study graph **E**.

  a Describe what has happened to the number of people who work in agriculture.

  b Describe what has happened to the number of people who work in manufacturing and services.

3 Write a short paragraph to summarise what you have found out about:

  a Changes in where people live.

  b Changes in jobs.

Case Study
What can we learn about China from the media?

A China Town in Liverpool

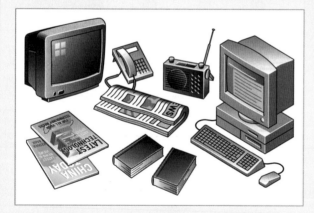

What is the media?

The **media** is any method of communication which reaches large numbers of people. Sometimes stories in the media are not the whole story. The story or image of a place or country often just reflects what the person writing the newspaper article, or making the TV programme, thinks about the country. How does China come across in the media? If you only knew about China from information in the media, what sort of place would you think it is?

Fact file

Technical achievements in ceramics

Chinese potters were making china that was fired to high temperatures of over 1200°C nearly 3500 years ago – the Shang dynasty. It took more than 3000 years before countries in the western world developed the technical expertise to make similar pots. High-fired, high-quality pottery is still called china. It is usually made from a type of very pure white clay called porcelain.

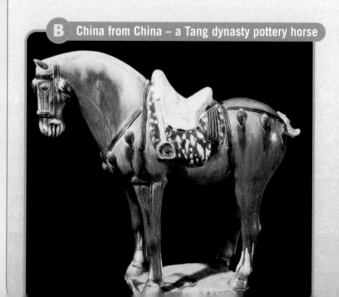

B China from China – a Tang dynasty pottery horse

China to build world's tallest dam

The Guardian, 15 May 2001

UK exporters fear Chinese uncertainty

The Times, 5 April 2001

China's dustbowl nightmare

The Guardian, 13 June 2001

China anger at British attacks on human rights

The Daily Telegraph, 1 December 2000

C What the papers say

Activities

1 Study photograph **A**.

   a What clues are there that this is China Town?

   b Do you think the area has grown up like this for local people *or* for tourists?

2 Read the fact file. What does it tell you about China in the past?

3 Study the newspaper headlines in **C**. Discuss with your teacher how China is reported to the British public.

4 Carry out an Internet search to find news articles on China. Through www.heinemann.co.uk/hotlinks, you could try the websites for:

   ⊚ BBC News

   ⊚ CNN News

   ⊚ Electronic Telegraph

   ⊚ Guardian Unlimited

   ⊚ Yahoo News **ICT**

1 Renminbi	= 100 Yuan
12 Renminbi	= £1

D Chinese currency

5 **Extension**

In the jaws of the Dragon

The Guardian, 3 April 2001

Why Dragon? The Chinese five-toed dragon is a symbol of happiness and good fortune. The Dragon stands for a wild, untamed, fierce creature in western cultures. The headline reflects an image of China as powerful (the jaws), mysterious and uncontrollable. In the West the headline is a threatening one. In China it would be difficult to understand. What does this say about the West's image of China? Why is it described in this way? Is China really like that?

China – the physical environment

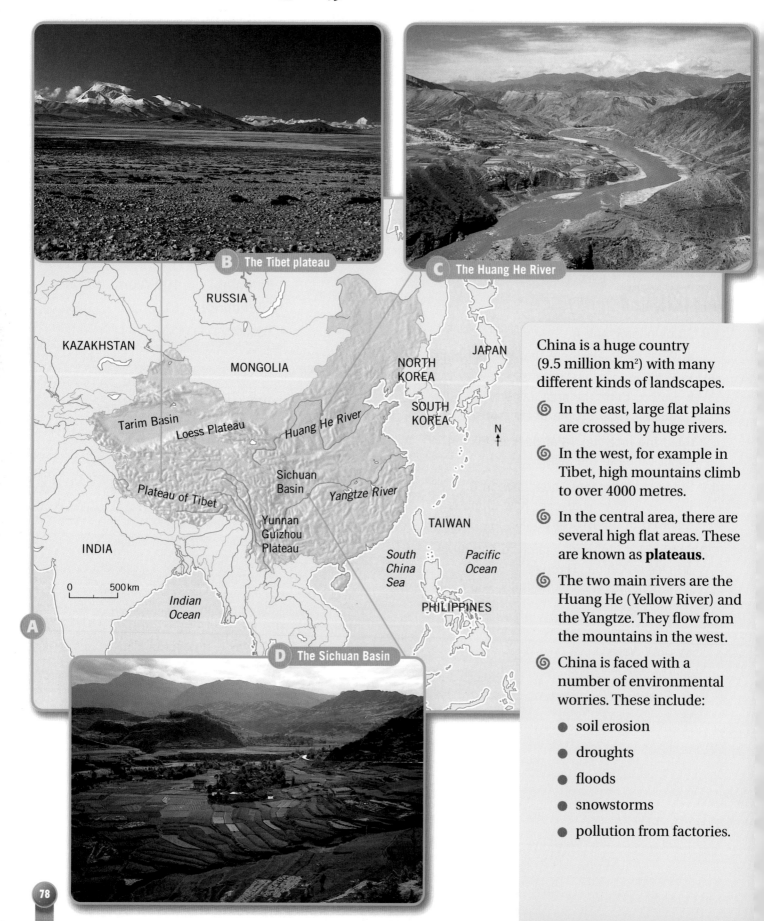

B The Tibet plateau

C The Huang He River

D The Sichuan Basin

RUSSIA

KAZAKHSTAN

MONGOLIA

JAPAN

NORTH KOREA

SOUTH KOREA

N

Tarim Basin

Loess Plateau

Huang He River

Plateau of Tibet

Sichuan Basin

Yangtze River

Yunnan Guizhou Plateau

INDIA

TAIWAN

South China Sea

Pacific Ocean

0   500 km

Indian Ocean

PHILIPPINES

A

China is a huge country (9.5 million km²) with many different kinds of landscapes.

- In the east, large flat plains are crossed by huge rivers.

- In the west, for example in Tibet, high mountains climb to over 4000 metres.

- In the central area, there are several high flat areas. These are known as **plateaus**.

- The two main rivers are the Huang He (Yellow River) and the Yangtze. They flow from the mountains in the west.

- China is faced with a number of environmental worries. These include:

  - soil erosion
  - droughts
  - floods
  - snowstorms
  - pollution from factories.

Flooding

In China each year flooding occurs on the Yangtze and Huang He rivers. In 1998 the worst flooding for 44 years occurred in Hubei province. Heavy rains in July and August formed a lake seven metres deep and covering nearly 325 km^2. More than 3000 people were killed, 2.9 million houses were destroyed and more than 9 million hectares of crops were ruined. Flood waters washed away a 3000-metre section of a newly built flood-protection dyke. Officials said that floods, landslides and mudflows affected some 240 million people – one fifth of China's population.

Fire

Forest fires during the hot dry season can cause severe damage. A total of 3021 people were killed and 4404 others injured in fires in China in 2000. Financial losses were more than 1.5 billion Yuan. The official Xinhua news agency said that tree felling as well as soil erosion following forest fires may have added to the flooding. Without the forest cover, rain flows quickly into the rivers, carrying large amounts of soil which silt up the river channels and cause flooding.

F   Earthquake damage at Zhangjiapo village, China

Earthquakes

China sits between two of the largest tectonic plate boundaries in the world. Since 1900 there have been more than 800 earthquakes measuring at least 6.0 on the Richter scale.

China has had some success with predicting earthquakes. Even so, since 1900 nearly half a million people have died in earthquakes. This is 53 per cent of the world's earthquake casualties.

On 10 January 1998 an earthquake of 6.2 on the Richter scale damaged more than nineteen cities and affected nearly 170 000 people in Zhangbei, Shangyi, Wanquan and Kangding. Forty-nine people were killed and 11 439 people were injured. The damage cost 794 million Yuan.

Activities

1. Discuss in class why the Chinese government has such a difficult task in protecting its citizens.

2. Does the British government face similar problems?

3. Choose one or more of the problems on this page. Write facts or figures about it under these headings:
   - when or where it happens
   - causes
   - effects.

Are there regional differences within China?

Some parts of China are very different from other parts of the country. But can you clearly identify these regions?

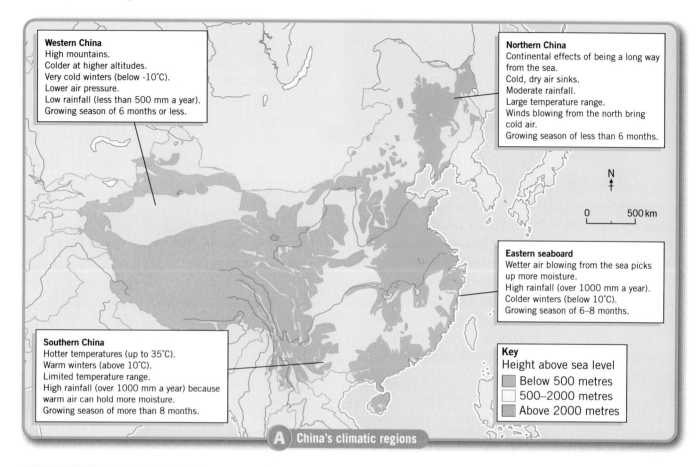

Western China
High mountains.
Colder at higher altitudes.
Very cold winters (below -10°C).
Lower air pressure.
Low rainfall (less than 500 mm a year).
Growing season of 6 months or less.

Northern China
Continental effects of being a long way from the sea.
Cold, dry air sinks.
Moderate rainfall.
Large temperature range.
Winds blowing from the north bring cold air.
Growing season of less than 6 months.

N

0   500 km

Eastern seaboard
Wetter air blowing from the sea picks up more moisture.
High rainfall (over 1000 mm a year).
Colder winters (below 10°C).
Growing season of 6–8 months.

Southern China
Hotter temperatures (up to 35°C).
Warm winters (above 10°C).
Limited temperature range.
High rainfall (over 1000 mm a year) because warm air can hold more moisture.
Growing season of more than 8 months.

Key
Height above sea level
Below 500 metres
500–2000 metres
Above 2000 metres

A China's climatic regions

What do we mean by a region?

Geographers often try to breakdown different parts of countries into *regions*. The idea is to show the features that make each area different. Of course, the real world does not always fit this idea of clear regions easily. For example, some features like climate or relief are easy to measure. Others, such as language differences, or political and economic differences, can be more difficult to identify. It is often difficult to know where one region ends and another begins – how do you draw lines in real places?

Activities

1. Map **A** shows detailed information on climate for four regions of China. Copy and complete the table below to summarise the climate in each region. Add figures if you can!

	Rainfall	Temperature	Growing season
Western China			
Southern China			
Eastern seaboard			
Northern China			

2. For each of the regions work out the height of the land above sea level. How do you think this affects the climate?

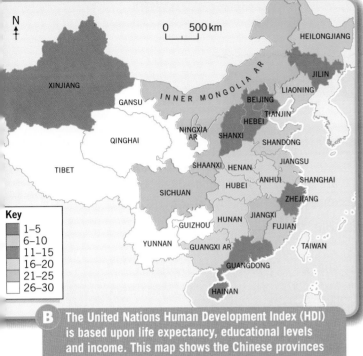

Key

	1–5
	6–10
	11–15
	16–20
	21–25
	26–30

B The United Nations Human Development Index (HDI) is based upon life expectancy, educational levels and income. This map shows the Chinese provinces ranked according to this index, where 1 is the best and 30 the worst

One country – two systems

In 1997 Hong Kong Island and the surrounding islands were returned to China as a Special Administrative Region (SAR). Some 6.2 million people live in the Hong Kong SAR. In the 1980s and 1990s Hong Kong developed a **democratic** system of government, which was one of the reasons why it has become a major economic centre. China still has a **centralised Communist** system of government. China calls this 'one country – two systems'.

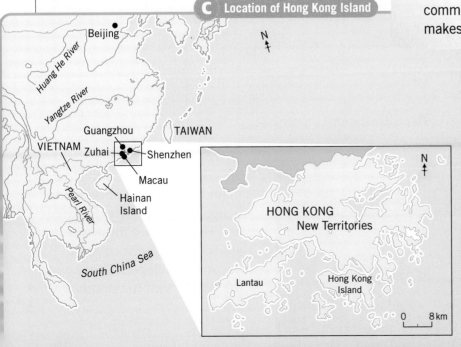

C Location of Hong Kong Island

Activities

1 **a** Study map **B** and work out which provinces have the best HDI.

b Now, look back at map **C** on page 74 showing population density. Are the provinces with the best HDI those that have low population densities or high population densities?

2 **a** On a base map of China, shade the three physical regions (lowlands, plateau and mountains).

b Make a series of three or four overlay maps. The first should show the areas of high population density and the major cities. What could you decide to show on the overlays – other climate, economic development, political provinces, HDI?

c Once you have completed your map and overlays, try to identify any different regions within China.

3 Which region of China would you like to live in? Explain your answer.

Getting Technical ▼

◉ A democratic system of government has the powerful leaders chosen or elected by the people. There are equal rights and privileges.

◉ A centralised Communist system of government is one where private property is abolished and all things are owned communally. The central committee becomes totally powerful and makes all the decisions.

D Hong Kong Island

Are there regional differences within Japan?

Just as Britain is divided into counties for local government, Japan is divided into 47 prefectures. These **prefectures** are then grouped into eight regions (map **A**).

Tohoku

Honshu Island has five regions. Tohoku is the furthest north. It is Japan's main rice-growing region. It has recently been linked to other regions by a new expressway and bullet train. Sendai is becoming a centre for industry and offices.

Hokkaido

The most northern island. Very few people live here. Jobs are mostly in farming and fishing, although tourism is becoming important.

A Japan's prefectures and regions

0   250 km

Chūbu

In the south along the Pacific coast it is mostly urban and industrial. The central mountainous areas are national parks that are easily accessible to many people. To the north, along the coast of the Sea of Japan, many nuclear power stations have been built.

Kyushu

The north of the island, which has very good links to Honshu, is an old industrial area. Two-thirds of the population of the island live here. The south is mainly farming, but it is also popular with tourists who come for the sub-tropical climate and volcanic scenery.

Shikoku

This is the smallest of the four main islands. New bridges are being built to connect Shikoku and Honshu, and these will allow the northern coast to become developed. The rest of the island is mountainous and remote.

Kanto

The largest concentration of population live in this region (see photo on page 70). Tokyo, the capital city, is a centre for manufacturing and service industries. The country's main port is at Yokohama. Kawasaki is one of the main areas for heavy industry. This region is sometimes called the 'heart' of Japan.

Chugoku

This region is remote and underdeveloped. The main city is Hiroshima. Inland it is mountainous.

Kinki

This is Japan's second most important industrial region. It contains three major cities: Kyoto, Osaka and Kobe.

Activities

1. Research photos of Shikoku and Kyushu from the Internet or a CD-ROM encyclopedia. Print each photo and annotate them from the information on page 82.

2. Use the photographs and information on these pages to list the physical and human features of the four islands of Hokkaido, Honshu, Shikoku and Kyushu. Copy the table below to help you to organise your ideas. Hokkaido has been started for you.

3. Choose two photographs which you think show the contrasts between the different regions in Japan. Draw a sketch of each photograph and add annotations to show the contrasts in physical and human features.

4. New road and rail links are planned to link Hokkaido with Honshu. How do you think this might change Hokkaido?

Island	Physical features	Human features
Hokkaido	The photograph shows ...	Few people ...
Honshu		
Shikoku		
Kyushu		

Japan – the physical environment

Most of Japan's islands are steep and mountainous so few people live here. There are four main islands and about 3900 smaller ones. In fact, less than sixteen per cent of the country is classed as lowland. It is in this small area of lowland that settlement and economic activity must take place. Flat land is a scarce resource in Japan (map **A**).

The steep mountains that make up the 'backbone' of the four main islands are the result of movements between the tectonic plates. When the plates move, the result is often an earthquake or volcanic activity. Sometimes underwater earthquakes cause huge waves called *tsunami*.

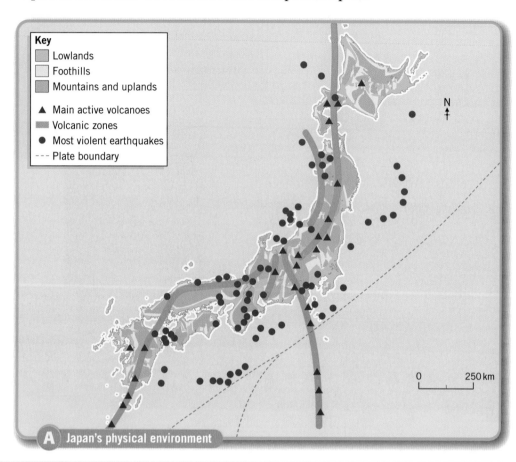

Key
- Lowlands
- Foothills
- Mountains and uplands
- ▲ Main active volcanoes
- Volcanic zones
- ● Most violent earthquakes
- --- Plate boundary

N

0   250 km

A Japan's physical environment

Activities

1. The physical environment of Japan has provided both opportunities and difficulties for the Japanese people. Copy and complete the table below to balance each of the opportunities with the difficulties people face.

2. **a** Read about the hazards Japan faces on page 85. Look back to page 79, and compare them with hazards in China.

b Make three lists:
- ⑥ Hazards in China and Japan
- ⑥ Hazards in China
- ⑥ Hazards in Japan.

Opportunities	Difficulties
Timber resources from the wooded mountains	Difficult to move around through thick forest on steep hillsides
Hot springs in the volcanic areas	
Wilderness areas with spectacular scenery to encourage tourists	
A good climate for growing crops	
Fishing in the coastal waters	

Earthquakes

Kobe (*left*) is the sixth largest city in Japan. On 17 January 1995 it was shaken by a series of earthquakes. The largest reached 7.2 on the Richter scale. It was Japan's worst earthquake for nearly 75 years. Nearly 6000 people were killed, some 26 000 were injured and up to 310 000 were left homeless. Some 75 000 buildings were damaged or destroyed. The repair bill was estimated at £60 billion.

Volcanoes

In September 2000 Mount Oyama erupted again (*right*), forcing residents to flee. Smoke rose as high as 3000 metres. Experts said it was the highest level of activity in recent years. About 630 people were ordered to leave the Tsubota and Kamitsuki areas. Here, a man tries to clean ash off his car.

Floods and landslides

In 1997 heavy rains triggered 200 mudslides. The village of Izumi was hardest hit. Here, 80 families lived in a valley known to be vulnerable to landslides. The government recognised the threat and started to build a 16-metre high concrete barrier. But it proved to be no protection. At 1 am on 16 July an avalanche of bright red mud, boulders and trees roared down the hill, crashing right through the barrier.

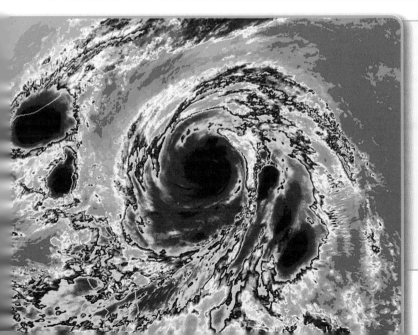

Typhoons

Typhoons (*left*) are like hurricanes. They develop in warm tropical waters and have winds of at least 65 kph. An average of 28 typhoons form between June and September each year, but usually only two or three pass across Japan. There have been few disasters recently because of improved forecasting techniques and better methods of warning people. The worst recent typhoon killed 19 people in September 1991.

Case Study

What can we learn about Japan from the media?

Word	How to draw/write	Kanji
Paddy field	亅冂冊用田	田
Tree	一十才木	木　木木 (Woods)　森 (Forest)
Mountain	㇑山山	山
River	㇇川川	川

A Japanese kanji

A major difference between Japan, China and western countries is the style of writing. Japanese writing developed from the Chinese system and in both systems the symbols represent something. The symbols are called **kanji**. Diagram **A** shows how some of these symbols have come about, and how to draw them. It is important to follow the arrows as these have been developed to ensure easy reading!

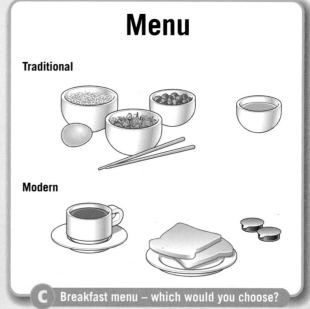

Menu

Traditional

Modern

C Breakfast menu – which would you choose?

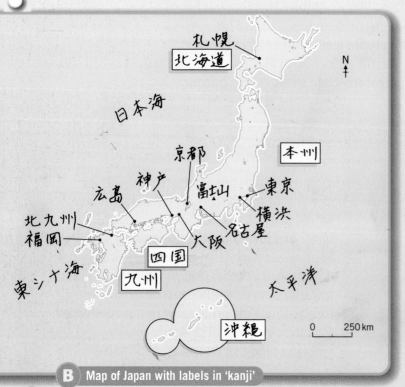

B Map of Japan with labels in 'kanji'

'Rice' and 'food' mean almost the same thing in Japan. Breakfast is literally translated as 'morning rice', while lunch would be 'noon rice' and dinner 'evening rice'. But like many other parts of Japanese life, peoples' views are changing. Few young people would choose the traditional breakfast menu from diagram **C** nowadays.

It has only been in the last 150 years that western people (for example those who live in Europe and North America) have become aware of Japan and the life of Japanese people.

Many features of Japanese life are mysterious and unfamiliar to us, for example art and religion.

In recent years, some parts of Japanese life have started to influence western people.

- ⑥ The Japanese language is taught in more and more British schools.

- ⑥ Japanese sports such as Kendo and Sumo wrestling are increasingly popular.

- ⑥ Many people relax using meditation techniques from the Buddhist religion.

- ⑥ Managers of factories study Japanese ways of working.

D Traditional Japanese art

E Urban living

Activities

① **a** Make a sketch map of a small, imaginary Japanese island. Label it using some of the kanji symbols in diagram **A**.

b How easy did you find it to write the kanji? Why do you think this is?

② Study photographs **D**, **E** and **F**.

a What can you learn from the photographs?

b List the ways in which the information in the photographs is incomplete.

c What photographs would you take to balance these pictures to make the image complete? Look through the pictures of Japan in this unit to help you with ideas.

③ **Extension**

Look for pictures from Japan showing scenes from the twenty-first century. Make your own poster showing your view of modern Japan.

F Traditional Japanese sword play demonstration

Trading places?

On 19 May 2000 China joined the World Trade Organisation (photograph **A**). Before China was allowed to join this organisation, European companies insisted on joining the fast-growing mobile phone industry in China.

Trade is vital to both China's and Japan's economic success. China's success as one of the world's largest trading nations is all the more remarkable because it has achieved this since 1978 when the **'open policy'** was declared. By 1997 China and Japan were each other's largest trading partner (diagram **B**), and both countries have economic links with the rest of the world.

But while China's economy has gone from strength to strength, Japan has suffered a 'slow down' in economic growth in the last ten years. In April 2000 the value of Japanese industries was lower than it had been in 1985. Consumers are spending less money, so to keep up any economic growth Japan has to trade with other countries. The result has been an increase in trade, investment and aid with China.

A China joins the World Trade Organisation

Getting Technical ▼

- **Exports** are goods or services that are sent out or sold to another country.
- **Invisible exports** are payments for services, for example earnings from transport, shipping, banking and tourism.
- **Visible exports** include items such as foodstuffs, raw materials and manufactured goods.
- **Imports** are goods and services that are brought in from another country through trade.
- **Balance of trade** is the difference in value between exports and imports. When a country exports more goods and services than it imports, it has a **trade surplus.**
- **Open policy** China's decision to open its doors to western businesses so that they could buy and sell things and information.

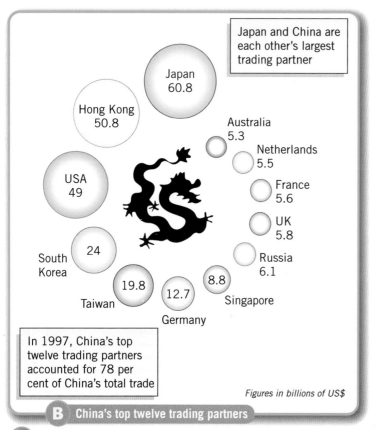

Japan and China are each other's largest trading partner

Japan 60.8
Hong Kong 50.8
USA 49
South Korea 24
Taiwan 19.8
Germany 12.7
Singapore 8.8
Russia 6.1
UK 5.8
France 5.6
Netherlands 5.5
Australia 5.3

In 1997, China's top twelve trading partners accounted for 78 per cent of China's total trade

Figures in billions of US$

B China's top twelve trading partners

C The top ten traders of the world

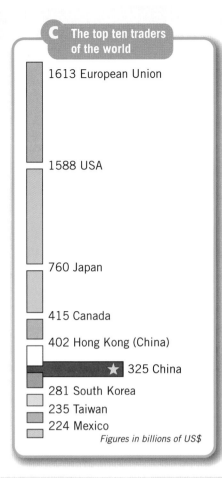

1613 European Union

1588 USA

760 Japan

415 Canada

402 Hong Kong (China)

★ 325 China

281 South Korea

235 Taiwan

224 Mexico

Figures in billions of US$

D The growth of China's exports and imports

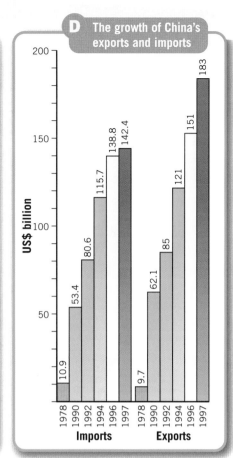

US$ billion

Imports:
- 1978: 10.9
- 1990: 53.4
- 1992: 80.6
- 1994: 115.7
- 1996: 138.8
- 1997: 142.4

Exports:
- 1978: 9.7
- 1990: 62.1
- 1992: 85
- 1994: 121
- 1996: 151
- 1997: 183

Imports **Exports**

Activities

1. Study graph **D**.

   a With your teacher, work out the balance of trade between China and the rest of the world for each year.

   b Write a sentence to describe what changes in trade the graph shows.

2. From what date has China had a trade surplus? What do you think China should spend this surplus on?

3. Study the information about Hong Kong here and on page 81. Write a short summary (no more than 30 words) to explain why Hong Kong is an important trading centre.

E Hong Kong

Hong Kong, a special administrative region

Hong Kong grew up because it was on a trade route and had a large, deep, sheltered harbour. It became part of China in 1997. The city is one of the world's most prosperous economies, and the population is growing rapidly. It is estimated that the number of people will increase from 6.7 million in 1999 to 8.2 million by 2015. Hong Kong is in the right place geographically and it is one of the main ports to import goods into mainland China. A new airport was recently built on Lantau island, which is linked to the mainland by road and rail bridges. A map to show the location of Hong Kong can be found on page 81.

What links do China and Japan have with the UK?

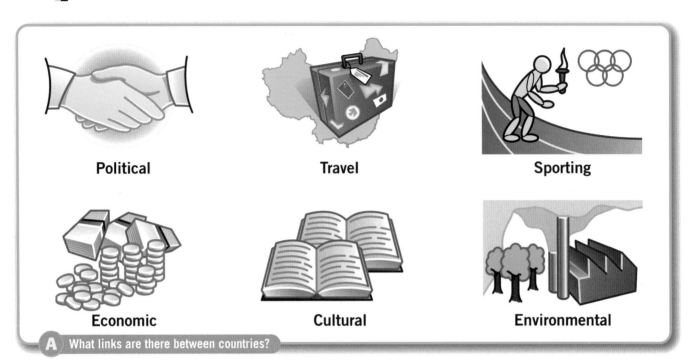

Political

Travel

Sporting

Economic

Cultural

Environmental

A What links are there between countries?

Japan has a long history of economic links with the UK. The UK is Japan's main trading partner in Europe, and many Japanese companies have built factories in the UK (diagram **B** and photograph **C**). Between 1997 and 2001 the Japanese economy grew very little. However, the Chinese economy continues to grow at a fast rate. Chinese exports were up by 28 per cent in 2000 and Chinese imports rose by 35 per cent.

Imports to the UK
from China in 2000
£5 005 million

Exports to China
from the UK in 2000
£1 468 million

C Japanese investment in high-tech factories in the UK (Mitsubishi, Scotland)

Imports to the UK
from Japan in 1999
£9 251 million

Exports to Japan
from the UK in 1999
£3 303 million

B Trade links between China, Japan and the UK

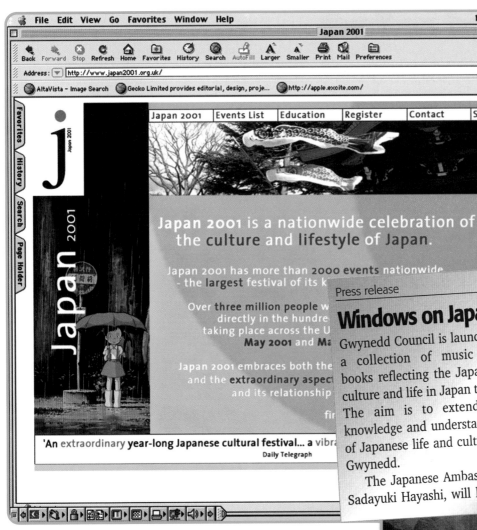

Japan 2001 is a nationwide celebration of the culture and lifestyle of Japan. Over two million people will take part in the hundreds of events taking place across the UK between May 2001 and March 2002. Japan 2001 celebrates both the ordinary and the extraordinary aspects of Japan and its links with the UK.

5 June 2001

Press release

Windows on Japan

Gwynedd Council is launching a collection of music and books reflecting the Japanese culture and life in Japan today. The aim is to extend the knowledge and understanding of Japanese life and culture in Gwynedd.

The Japanese Ambassador, Sadayuki Hayashi, will launch the collection at Bangor Library on Saturday 9 June. The collection will tour Gwynedd's main libraries during the year.

Gwynedd Council has been working with the staff of the Institute of Japanese Studies, University of Wales, Bangor on this venture.

D Cultural links between Japan and the UK

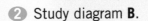

E Travel links between China and the UK

Activities

1 Study box **D**, which shows some of the cultural links between the UK and Japan.

a Ask your teacher to explain cultural links.

b Why do you think Gwynedd Council in North Wales has set up the collection of books and music?

c What do you think the Japan 2001 series of cultural events hopes to achieve? Why are events such as these important?

d i Choose one other type of link shown in diagram **A** and make a list of the activities and events that could be organised to strengthen this link.

ii How would Japan and the UK benefit from these activities?

2 Study diagram **B**.

a In a group, work out the balance of trade between the UK and China and the UK and Japan.

b If the economy of Japan is not growing and the economy of China is growing, what would you expect to happen to the trade between the UK and these countries in the future?

c Do you think Chinese factories similar to the Japanese one in photograph **C** will be built in the UK? Explain your answer.

Review and reflect

Activities

1 Look back at the list of ten questions you wrote down for question **1c** on page 71.

   a Have you found answers to them all?

   b Now you know more about Japan and China, would you like to change any of your questions? If so, which questions would you ask instead?

   c What sort of information was the hardest to find?

2 Look back at the photographs on pages 70–71. Captions to the photographs are given here with the country. How many of your choices were correct?

C Great Wall of China

China

F Farmer in Nagano-ken

Japan

D Beijing centre

China

G NKK steelworks

Japan

E Main road in Tokyo

Japan

H Volkswagen car plant, Shanghai

China

3 Now you have collected your information, you can start to plan your report to compare Japan and China. Diagram **A** reminds you about the steps you need to take when carrying out a geographical enquiry.

You need to present your findings in the form of a report. There are many ways of doing this, not all of them written. Diagram **B** shows some ideas.

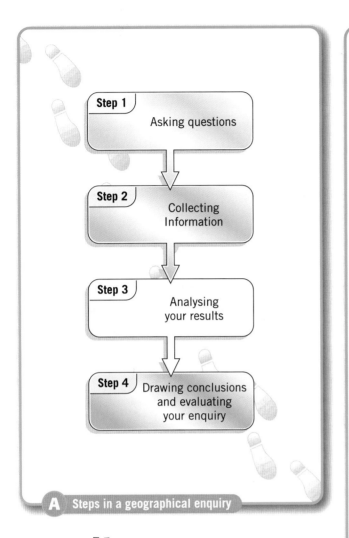

A Steps in a geographical enquiry

Step 1 Asking questions

Step 2 Collecting Information

Step 3 Analysing your results

Step 4 Drawing conclusions and evaluating your enquiry

Written report   **Spoken report**   **Wall display**

Microsoft PowerPoint presentation

Published on a website

Radio documentary

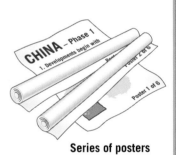

Series of posters

B Reporting back

How to ...

The following ideas will help you write your report.

◉ *Introduction*: Which countries were you studying? Where are they?

◉ *Data used*: What kinds of data did you use to find out about life in these two countries?

◉ *Explanation*: What were the main things you found out about China? What were the main things you found out about Japan?

◉ *Conclusion*: How are the two countries similar? How are the two countries different?

◉ *Evaluation*: Which parts of your enquiry were easy? Which parts of your enquiry were difficult?

6 Virtual volcanoes and earthquakes

A Stromboli – Station 14

B Aerial photograph of Stromboli

Italy

Stromboli

Sicily

N

0   100 km

C Location of Stromboli

Learn about

In this unit you are going to learn about

- tectonic patterns and processes
- the impact of these processes on countries that are at different stages of economic development
- how to use the Internet to carry out enquiries about volcanoes and earthquakes.

A virtual field trip up Stromboli

Stromboli is a volcanic island located between Sicily and the Italian mainland. It is one of the most active volcanoes on Earth. It has been in nearly continuous eruption for around 2000 years. The island is about 2 km in diameter. Its highest point is 924 metres above sea level but it rises over 3000 metres above the floor of the Tyrrhenian Sea.

In 1991 the population of the island was 361. However, during the summer months there are many more people, mainly due to tourism.

D The area around Stromboli

Activities

Imagine that your class is going on a one week geography field trip to study Stromboli, an active volcano. Carry out some research using the website: 'Stromboli Online' at www.heinemann.co.uk/hotlinks. (123) (ICT)

1 a Collect information using these headings:
- Population and settlement
- Transport
- Shops
- Weather and climate
- Vegetation
- Tourist information
- Health and safety (including possible hazards).

b When do you think is the best time of year to carry out the field trip?

c What else do you need to know in order to plan, and why?

2 Choose the items you should carry up the volcano in your rucksack. To carry it comfortably, your backpack should weigh no more than 7.5 kg. Table **E** lists the possible items to choose from and their weights. To help you make sensible choices, use your research from question 1.

3 Carry out a *virtual field trip* at 'Stromboli Online'.

a Before you begin, check out today's weather conditions using links from the website to both satellite images and weather stations (Napoli is the nearest).

b Choose whichever virtual route you prefer. As you go up the volcano, collect the following information:
- the altitude at each station
- photographs
- at least one labelled field sketch
- changing vegetation types.

4 At the end of the field trip reconsider your rucksack contents. Which were the good and poor choices? Why?

Contents	Weight	Contents	Weight
2 litres bottled water	2 kg	Suntan lotion	200 g
Food for one day	1.5 kg	Sandals	200 g
Trainers	800 g	Clipboard	200 g
Binoculars	800 g	Spare T-shirt	200 g
Jumper	700 g	Hat	150 g
Fleece	600 g	Insect repellent	100 g
Roll mat	500 g	Swimsuit / trunks	100 g
First aid kit	500 g	Map	50 g
Rucksack	500 g	Pencils	50 g
Camera and film	500 g	Money bag	50 g
Flask of hot drink	400 g	Compass	50 g
Towel	300 g	Sunglasses	50 g
Waterproof	300 g	Change of socks	50 g
Thermals	300 g	Change of underwear	50 g
Trowel	300 g		
Shorts	250 g		

E Items that you might need on your trip

95

What are volcanoes? Are they all the same?

What causes volcanoes?

Deep within the Earth it is so hot that some rocks melt to become a thick flowing substance called **magma**.

 Volcanoes are openings in the Earth's surface through which magma and ash erupt onto the land.

 Magma that has erupted is called **lava**.

 Some volcanic eruptions are explosive and others are not. It depends on how runny or sticky the magma is.

Lava flows

If magma is thin and runny, gases can escape from it so that it flows easily out of the volcano. Lava flows rarely kill anyone, because they move slowly enough for people to get out of their way, but they can destroy buildings in their path.

A Some features of a volcano

Volcanic bombs, ash and gases thrown into the air

Main vent

Crater – the funnel-shaped hollow at the top of the vent

Lava flow

Volcanic cone

Layers of lava and ash built up over repeated eruptions

Parasitic cone

Magma chamber – a store of molten rock inside the Earth

Explosive eruptions

 If magma is viscous (thick) gases cannot escape easily. Pressure builds up until the gases escape violently and explode. In this type of eruption, the magma blasts into the air and breaks apart into pieces called *volcanic bombs*.

 Explosive volcanic eruptions can be dangerous and deadly. They cause fiery clouds which race down mountainsides, destroying everything in their path.

 When hot volcanic materials mix with water from streams, *lahars* (mudflows) form. These can bury entire settlements.

Types of volcanoes

There are many different ways to *classify* volcanoes. One is based on the shape of the volcanic landform. The most common types are:

 strato volcanoes (sometimes called *composite*)

 shield volcanoes.

Volcanoes of a third, less common type, **caldera complexes**, are huge and very explosive. They often do not even look like volcanoes because when they do erupt they collapse in on themselves. The last major caldera complex eruption was Taupo in 83 AD.

Strato volcanoes

Strato volcanoes make up 60 per cent of the Earth's volcanoes and are formed from layers of lava and ash. Their lava tends to be thick and flows very slowly. This causes them to form steep-sided volcanic domes. The thick lava also allows gas pressures to build up, causing explosive eruptions. Examples of strato volcanoes include Mount St Helens, Stromboli, Pinatubo, Mount Fuji, Merapi, Arenal and Cotopaxi.

B Arenal, Costa Rica

Shield volcanoes

Shield volcanoes are the largest volcanoes on Earth. Shield volcanoes erupt lava that is very fluid. For this reason these volcanoes are not steep – the lava runs downhill too easily to form a pile. They also have very broad bases. Eruptions at shield volcanoes mainly consist of fountains of lava and lava flows. The Hawaiian shield volcanoes, Kilauea and Mauna Loa, are famous examples.

C Mauna Loa, Hawaii

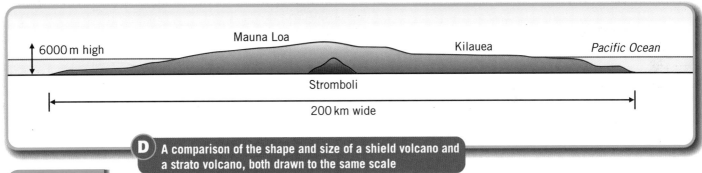

D A comparison of the shape and size of a shield volcano and a strato volcano, both drawn to the same scale

Activities

1. Carry out an Internet enquiry into the characteristics of volcanoes across the world using the website 'Volcano World' at www.heinemann.co.uk/hotlinks. Draw a table in Word, like the one below, into which you can copy and paste your information. Add an extra column for satellite images and photographs if you wish. Begin with the volcanoes named on these two pages. (ICT)

Name of volcano	Location Country	Continent	Height	Type	Date of last eruption	Number of deaths	Features of eruptions
Stromboli	Italy	Europe	924 m	Strato	Continuous	4 in 1919 4 in 1930 4 in 1986	Small gas explosions with blobs of lava thrown up. Explosions each hour.

2. Create a word bank with definitions for the vocabulary you have included in your table.

3. Plot the location of each of your volcanoes onto a blank world map.

What are earthquakes?
Are they all the same?

Case Study

The information on pages 98 and 99 is from the *BBC Online* website. It is a small selection of the news reports following the Gujarat earthquake which struck India in January 2001.

Fact file: Gujarat, January 2001

- ◎ **Time and date:** 8.46 am local time on 26 January 2001.
- ◎ **Strength:** 7.9 on the Richter Scale – India's biggest earthquake since 1956. Tremors were felt as far away as Bangladesh.
- ◎ **Epicentre:** Near the town of Bhuj in Gujarat state, north-west India.
- ◎ **Level of Economic Development:** India is an **LEDC** (Less Economically Developed Country).

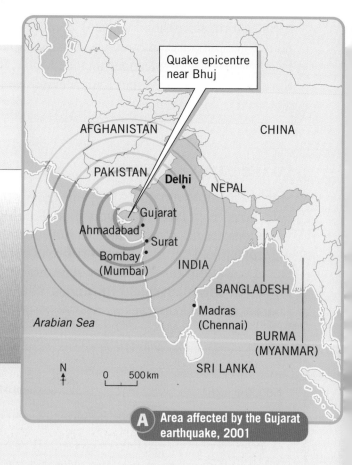

A Area affected by the Gujarat earthquake, 2001

What happened during the earthquake?

Dear Viki

I was just getting up and suddenly felt that a large group of monkeys were running around in the terrace because the room was shaking. The shakings didn't stop and became more severe. It was then that I suspected something big on the lines of an earthquake, but I couldn't believe it because Ahmadabad had never been hit by one.

I cannot describe the shaking to you. Just imagine how you would feel if someone very powerful took hold of your house and started shaking it right from the foundations. After about a minute it stopped. I have been lucky, by God's grace.

Vivek

B An e-mail from Vivek Iyer, an Ahmadabad doctor

The effects on buildings and infrastructure

Many lives could have been saved in the Gujarat earthquake if building codes had been enforced and cheap protection measures carried out, Indian scientists say.

One civil engineer from Bombay said: 'We are beginning to learn that governments are not prepared. They directly or indirectly contribute to the deaths by allowing poor construction quality.'

India, along with other developing countries, has fast growing cities, so buildings are being put up quickly to meet growing housing needs. Some developers, keen to make a quick profit, are not as worried about safety as they should be.

C

• The effects on the people •

At least 30 000 people are estimated to have died in the quake. Another 55 000 have been injured and about half a million made homeless.

As hopes of finding survivors fade, aid agencies are now trying to provide food, shelter and water to the families without homes.

Efforts are focusing on the need to cremate the thousands of dead to prevent the spread of disease. Many hospitals are treating people in the open air, and doctors say they are running out of bandages and medical supplies.

D News report, 30 January 2001

F Earthquake fault, Gujarat

E A young earthquake victim

Short-term responses to the earthquake

Aid from around the world has been pouring into India's earthquake zone. In a rare act, a plane from India's long-time rival Pakistan arrived carrying 2500 blankets and 200 tents for the quake survivors.

The United Nations Children's Fund has committed at least US $8 million in immediate aid. They have delivered thousands of blankets, a million chlorine tablets for purifying water, and plastic sheeting for shelter.

G News report, 1 February 2001

The effects on the economy

The cost of India's quake

Gujarat is India's second largest industrial region, with many steel and textile mills. It has India's busiest port, Kandla. Repairing buildings and installations is expected to cost around 150 billion rupees (£2.2 billion). It is an expense that India can ill afford. The government has asked the World Bank for a £1.1 billion loan to aid the rebuilding.

Industries hit

The diamond, pharmaceuticals and textile industries are likely to be worst hit by the massive disruption to power lines, transport and telecommunications. Jobs will be lost.

H News report, 2 February 2001

---

2 Present your earthquake case study under the following headings:
- What happened
- Effects on buildings and infrastructure
- Effects on the people
- Effects on the economy
- Short and long term responses

3 Add the geographical terms you have used to your word bank.

4 Compare your earthquake case study with those of others in your class.

5 Plot the locations of each of the earthquake case studies onto the same world outline map as your volcanoes in the activities on page 97.

Activities

You can find the BBC online website at www.heinemann.co.uk/hotlinks
Follow the links to *one* recent earthquake to produce a *case study* like this one. ICT

1 Produce a fact file like the one on page 98 to introduce your earthquake case study.

Where do earthquakes and volcanoes occur?

Activities ICT

Map **A** was taken from the earthquake area of the National Earthquake Information Centre website. Answer these questions using the map and an atlas.

1. In which country was the most recent earthquake event?

2. What was the strength and depth of this earthquake?

3. What was the depth of the deepest recent earthquake? In which country did it happen

4. What was the strength of the strongest earthquake? In which country did it happen?

5. Did any of these earthquakes make the news in the UK? If so, why?

6. Now download today's national earthquake map from the United States Geological Survey (see www.heinemann.co.uk/hotlinks). Use this map to answer questions **1–5** above.

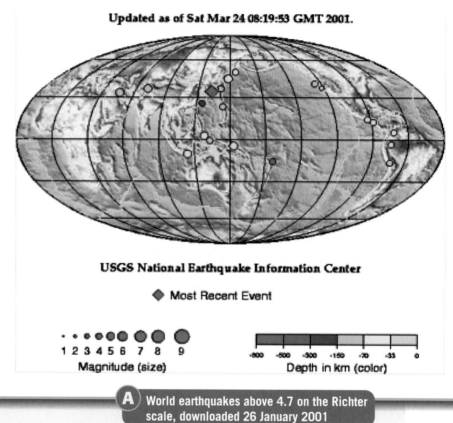

Updated as of Sat Mar 24 08:19:53 GMT 2001.

USGS National Earthquake Information Center

◆ Most Recent Event

1 2 3 4 5 6 7 8 9
Magnitude (size)

-800 -500 -300 -150 -70 -33 0
Depth in km (color)

A World earthquakes above 4.7 on the Richter scale, downloaded 26 January 2001

The Earth's crust is divided into about fifteen segments called **tectonic plates**. These plates 'float' on the mantle. Heat from within the Earth creates movements in the mantle. These cause the tectonic plates to move slowly, sometimes only a few centimetres per year.

Plates can move towards, away from or past one another. The boundaries where the plates meet are called **plate margins**. These are **active zones** because this is where most of the world's earthquakes and volcanic eruptions occur. There are two types of crust.

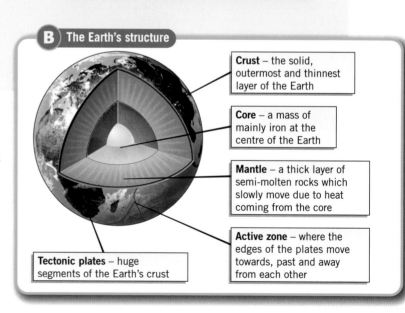

B The Earth's structure

Crust – the solid, outermost and thinnest layer of the Earth

Core – a mass of mainly iron at the centre of the Earth

Mantle – a thick layer of semi-molten rocks which slowly move due to heat coming from the core

Active zone – where the edges of the plates move towards, past and away from each other

Tectonic plates – huge segments of the Earth's crust

- *Continental crust* is lighter, thick (35–70 km) and very old (over 1500 million years).
- *Oceanic crust* is heavier, thin (6–10 km) and young (mostly less than 200 million years).

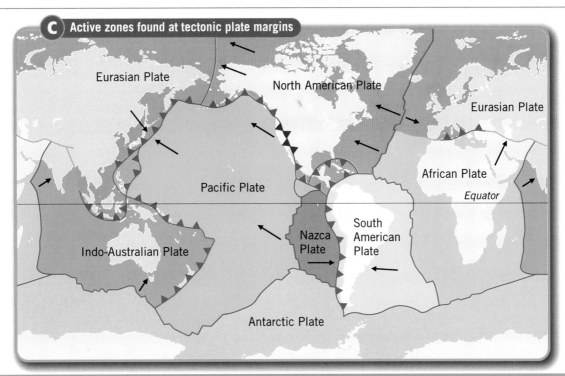

C Active zones found at tectonic plate margins

Type of plate margin	Description of what happens
Constructive margin ———	Two plates move away from each other and magma rises to the surface to form new crust.
Destructive margin	Oceanic crust moves towards continental crust but, being heavier, it sinks beneath the continental rock and is destroyed.
Collision zone	Plates made of continental crust move towards each other. They cannot sink so they crumple upwards to form **fold mountains.**
Conservative margin	Two plates move past each other. Crust is neither formed nor destroyed.

Activities

Compare your world map of earthquake and volcano locations from the activities on pages 97 and 99 with map **C** above.

1. On what types of plate margin do earthquakes tend to happen?

2. On what types of plate margin do volcanoes tend to erupt?

3. Use a world physical map in an atlas to name two fold mountain ranges at collision zones.

4. The Andes are also fold mountains.

   a. On which type of plate margin are they located?

   b. Name the two plates which are causing the Andes to form.

What causes earthquakes and volcanoes?

Active zones at destructive plate margins

Active zones at destructive margins occur where a plate made of oceanic crust moves towards a plate made of continental crust. The oceanic crust is heavier, so it is forced beneath the lighter continental crust and forms a **deep sea trench**. Because the plates do not slide smoothly past one another, there is often a huge build-up of tension. If the crust breaks, shock waves are sent out in all directions. This is called an earthquake. The point where the crust breaks is called the **focus**. The place where the shock waves reach the Earth's surface is called the **epicentre**.

As the oceanic crust pushes beneath the continental crust, it melts. This is partly due to the heat caused by friction between the plates and partly due to the increase in temperature as it reaches the mantle. This creates magma which escapes to the surface along lines of weakness in the Earth's crust called **faults** to form volcanoes. Volcanic eruptions at destructive plate margins can be very violent.

A Stromboli erupting

Case Study

What caused Stromboli to form?

Stromboli has formed as a result of repeated volcanic eruptions which have built up layers of lava and ash to create a **strato volcano**. These eruptions are caused by the movement of the *African Plate* and the *Eurasian Plate* towards each other. As the *African Plate* is forced beneath the lighter *Eurasian Plate*, it heats up and melts. If the pressure on this magma builds up, it eventually rises to the Earth's surface to form volcanoes such as *Vesuvius*, *Etna* and *Stromboli*. The movement of these two plates towards one another also causes the crust to crumple upwards to form fold mountains such as the *Atlas Mountains* in North Africa and the *Apennines* in Italy.

B A destructive margin

NORTH   SOUTH

Mt Vesuvius
Stromboli   *Mediterranean Sea*
SICILY
Apennines   *Tyrrhenian*   Mount Etna
(fold mountains)   *Sea*   Atlas Mountains
ITALIAN   (fold mountains)
MAINLAND   NORTH AFRICA

Sea level

Magma rises along fault
lines to form volcanoes
EURASIAN CRUST   Deep sea   AFRICAN PLATE
(continental crust)   trench   (continental crust)

The crust is heated as it is
forced towards the mantle
and melts to form magma

Collision zones

An area where two plates made of continental crust move towards one another is called a **collision zone**. Because neither plate can sink beneath the other, their crust is crumpled upwards to form **fold mountains**, such as the Himalayas. These mountains are still increasing in height as the Indian Plate moves into the Eurasian Plate at a rate of about 5 cm per year, as measured using satellite images. Sometimes, as with destructive margins, tension may build up over time. Eventually the crust will break, sending out shock waves – an earthquake.

Conservative plate margins

At conservative margins two plates move past one another, as in the case of the North American and Pacific Plates on the west coast of California (see **D**). Although the plates are travelling in the same direction, the Pacific Plate is moving faster, causing the plate margins to 'grind' past each other.

Case Study

What caused the Gujarat earthquake, 26 January 2001?

The earthquake which hit *Gujarat State* in *north-east India* on *26 January 2001* was caused by the *Indian Plate* moving *north* towards the *Eurasian Plate* (see **C**). As both plates are made of continental crust, neither can sink so they crumple upwards. This causes tension to build up in the *Eurasian Plate*. This strain eventually made the crust break, causing an earthquake with a focus at a shallow depth of *16 km*. The epicentre was close to the town of *Bhuj*.

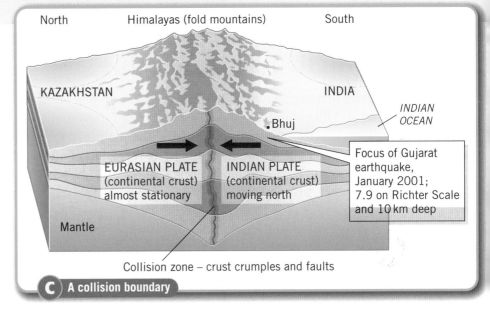

North   Himalayas (fold mountains)   South

KAZAKHSTAN   INDIA

INDIAN OCEAN

.Bhuj

EURASIAN PLATE (continental crust) almost stationary

INDIAN PLATE (continental crust) moving north

Focus of Gujarat earthquake, January 2001; 7.9 on Richter Scale and 10 km deep

Mantle

Collision zone – crust crumples and faults

C   A collision boundary

As with destructive margins, when the two plates 'stick' it causes tension to build up. When this tension is suddenly released an earthquake occurs. Earthquakes happen daily along the San Andreas fault, but major events, causing loss of life, are much less frequent. The 1994 Los Angeles earthquake measured 6.6 on the Richter Scale and caused 60 deaths. At conservative margins, crust is neither created nor destroyed, so volcanic eruptions do not occur.

D   The San Andreas fault, California, USA

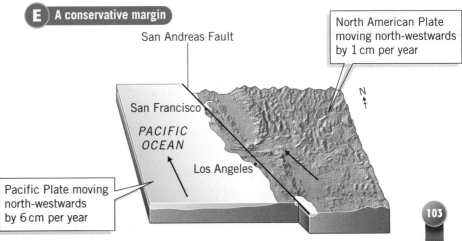

E   A conservative margin

San Andreas Fault

North American Plate moving north-westwards by 1 cm per year

San Francisco

PACIFIC OCEAN

Los Angeles

Pacific Plate moving north-westwards by 6 cm per year

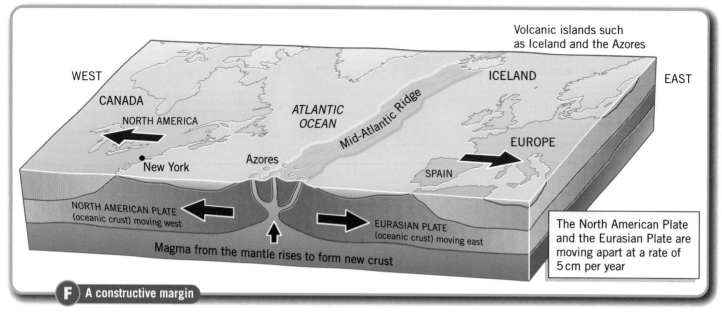

WEST

CANADA
NORTH AMERICA

ATLANTIC OCEAN

New York

Azores

Mid-Atlantic Ridge

Volcanic islands such as Iceland and the Azores

ICELAND

EUROPE

SPAIN

EAST

NORTH AMERICAN PLATE
(oceanic crust) moving west

EURASIAN PLATE
(oceanic crust) moving east

Magma from the mantle rises to form new crust

The North American Plate and the Eurasian Plate are moving apart at a rate of 5 cm per year

F A constructive margin

Constructive plate margins

At constructive margins two plates move away from one another, as in the case of the North American and Eurasian Plates (see **F**). This type of movement happens mostly under oceans. As the plates move apart magma rises from the mantle to form new oceanic crust. This creates a line of underwater volcanoes along the plate margins called a **mid oceanic ridge**. In places the volcanoes become large enough to appear above sea level as volcanic islands such as Iceland. The type of volcano most often formed at a constructive plate margin is a shield volcano.

Activities

1 What causes a volcanic eruption?

Choose one of the volcanoes you studied when you carried out your Internet Enquiry on page 97. Carry out the following activities based on that volcano.

a Name the type of plate margin on which the volcano is located using figure **D** on page 101.

b Draw a large labelled diagram (A4 size) to show how this volcano was formed. Use diagram **B** on page 102 or diagram **F** on this page for guidance.

⑥ Use an atlas to name actual places and features on your diagram, e.g. countries, plates, mountain ranges.

⑥ Make sure that you use the correct key words in your annotations.

⑥ Give your diagram a title – include in it the name of the volcano and the type of plate margin.

c The Case Study boxes on pages 102 and 103 show how to explain the causes of volcanic eruptions and earthquakes. Use these to help you to write a paragraph explaining how the volcano you have drawn was caused.

Make sure you:

⑥ use the correct key words – these appear in **bold print** in this unit

⑥ name actual places and features which are specific to the location of your volcano – these appear in *italics* in the Case Study boxes.

2 What causes an earthquake?

Carry out the following activities based on the earthquake in your case study (page 99).

a Name the type of plate margin on which the earthquake happened. Use figure **D** on page 101.

b Draw a large labelled diagram (A4 size) to show why this earthquake occurred. Use diagrams **B**, **C** and **E** on pages 102–104 and the bullet points in activity **1b** opposite for guidance.

c Write a paragraph explaining how the earthquake you have drawn was caused. Use the bullet points in activity **1c** to help you.

How do people live with earthquakes and volcanoes?

We expect earthquakes to happen but some earthquake disasters need not. Scientists and engineers are working to understand earthquake hazards and to help people to prepare for future earthquakes, especially in active zones which are very densely populated. They can try to predict the earthquake, and reduce the damage by being better prepared.

How can earthquakes be predicted?

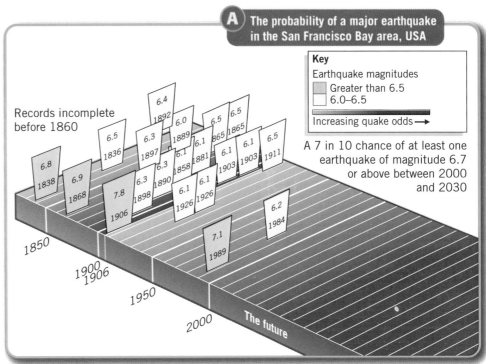

A The probability of a major earthquake in the San Francisco Bay area, USA

Records incomplete before 1860

Key
Earthquake magnitudes
Greater than 6.5
6.0–6.5
Increasing quake odds →

A 7 in 10 chance of at least one earthquake of magnitude 6.7 or above between 2000 and 2030

6.8 1838
6.9 1868
6.5 1836
7.8 1906
6.3 1897
6.3 1898
6.3 1890
6.4 1892
6.0 1889
6.1 1858
6.1 1881
6.5 1865
6.5 1865
6.1 1903
6.1 1903
6.5 1911
6.1 1926
6.1 1926
6.2 1984
7.1 1989

1850
1900 1906
1950
2000
The future

If scientists can predict when and where an earthquake will happen, people can be warned and lives saved, so scientists **monitor** (study) active zones.

- Sensitive instruments measure earth movements and check the strain building up in rocks.

- The number of earthquakes can be plotted to show if a major earthquake is likely. Figure **A** shows that a major earthquake is expected around San Francisco Bay in the next thirty years.

- Several earthquakes often strike in a short time. **Foreshocks** occur before some large earthquakes, so scientists can work out the chances of a larger **mainshock** following. In August 1989 a shock of magnitude 5.1 struck near San Francisco. The public was warned that a larger quake could follow. Sixty-nine days later, 63 people were killed by the Loma Prieta quake, magnitude 7.1.

- **Hazard shaking maps** (see **B**) show the risk of earthquakes. They can help governments to plan emergency services and earthquake education. Engineers can plan earthquake codes for buildings, bridges and roads.

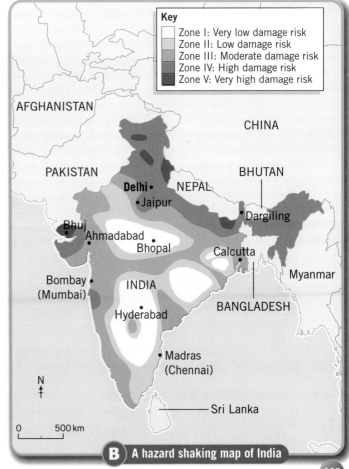

Key
Zone I: Very low damage risk
Zone II: Low damage risk
Zone III: Moderate damage risk
Zone IV: High damage risk
Zone V: Very high damage risk

AFGHANISTAN
CHINA
PAKISTAN
BHUTAN
Delhi
NEPAL
Jaipur
Dargiling
Bhuj
Ahmadabad
Bhopal
Calcutta
Myanmar
Bombay (Mumbai)
INDIA
BANGLADESH
Hyderabad
Madras (Chennai)
N
Sri Lanka
0   500 km

B A hazard shaking map of India

How can people prepare for earthquakes?

Building codes

Many people are killed when earthquakes destroy buildings. Scientists can test how buildings respond to quakes, and improve their ability to survive by using shake tables or platforms. The world's largest shake table is in Tsukuba Science City, Japan. It can carry buildings of up to 300 tonnes. Photo **C** shows a smaller shake table being used to test houses in India. Houses are built on a platform mounted on rollers, which is shaken by a tractor. The building on the right of the photo, made with cement mortar, collapses but the other, built with mud mortar, survives.

C A low-cost shake table in Latur, India

Education

People in Japan practice earthquake drills every year on 'Disaster Day' – 1 September. Similar drills are carried out in other places where earthquakes are a hazard, for example by practising DROP, COVER, AND HOLD ON (see the Red Cross website at www.heinemann.co.uk/hotlinks).

Emergency services and relief

Governments must plan carefully to make sure the emergency services are prepared for possible earthquakes, and that relief supplies are ready. Good communication with earthquake monitoring stations can also save lives. This may be a problem for countries that cannot afford monitoring equipment and sophisticated communications.

D The Transamerica Pyramid in San Francisco, USA was designed to withstand earthquakes

Activities ICT

The information on pages 105 and 106 is about how people predict and prepare for earthquakes to try to reduce their effects. Carry out an Internet enquiry into how people predict and prepare for volcanic eruptions.

- Answer the questions using the websites and links available at www.heinemann.co.uk/hotlinks.
- Include case study information and illustrations.

How can volcanic eruptions be predicted?

1. How can volcanoes be monitored?
2. What signs suggest a volcano may soon erupt?

How can people prepare for volcanic eruptions?

3. How are eruption warnings given?
4. How can the public be better informed about volcanic hazards?
5. What should people do if a volcano erupts?

help!

- Type the enquiry questions into a Word document.
- Copy and paste relevant information from the websites under each question.
- Highlight in red the most relevant information, then delete the rest.
- Put the text into a logical order.
- Insert side headings for each section of information.

Review and reflect

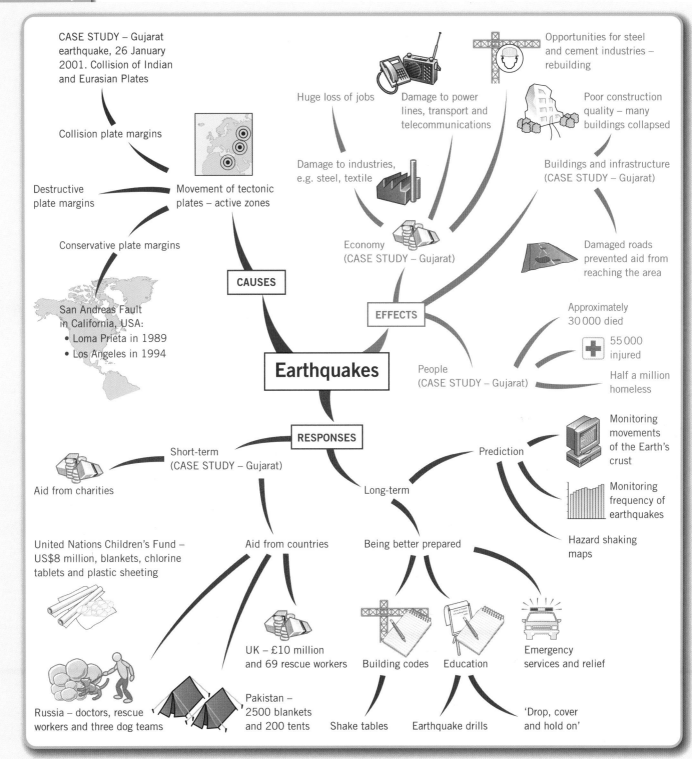

CASE STUDY – Gujarat earthquake, 26 January 2001. Collision of Indian and Eurasian Plates

Collision plate margins

Destructive plate margins

Conservative plate margins

Movement of tectonic plates – active zones

San Andreas Fault in California, USA:
- Loma Prieta in 1989
- Los Angeles in 1994

CAUSES

Earthquakes

RESPONSES

Huge loss of jobs

Damage to power lines, transport and telecommunications

Damage to industries, e.g. steel, textile

Economy (CASE STUDY – Gujarat)

EFFECTS

People (CASE STUDY – Gujarat)

Opportunities for steel and cement industries – rebuilding

Poor construction quality – many buildings collapsed

Buildings and infrastructure (CASE STUDY – Gujarat)

Damaged roads prevented aid from reaching the area

Approximately 30 000 died

55 000 injured

Half a million homeless

Short-term (CASE STUDY – Gujarat)

Aid from charities

United Nations Children's Fund – US$8 million, blankets, chlorine tablets and plastic sheeting

Aid from countries

Long-term

Being better prepared

Prediction

Monitoring movements of the Earth's crust

Monitoring frequency of earthquakes

Hazard shaking maps

Russia – doctors, rescue workers and three dog teams

UK – £10 million and 69 rescue workers

Pakistan – 2500 blankets and 200 tents

Building codes

Education

Shake tables

Earthquake drills

Emergency services and relief

'Drop, cover and hold on'

The mind map above shows a summary of the earthquake information covered in this unit. Use it as a model to draw a similar mind map for the volcano information you have collected. You should begin with the heading VOLCANOES in the centre and the three sub-headings of CAUSES, EFFECTS and RESPONSES. Add the facts from your own research as well as including information from the textbook.

7 Cars on the Internet

The global car industry

Making cars is one of the world's growth industries. In 2000, sales for passenger cars around the world rose to 49.4 million, the highest ever. The demand for all vehicles, including trucks and vans, increased to 58.2 million. As graph **A** shows, sales of new cars have grown steadily over the past twenty years. However, car sales and the factories where cars are made are unevenly distributed around the world (table **B** and map **C**).

A Car sales, 1983–2000

Unit Sales (million): axis 0–50

1984 86 88 90 92 94 96 98 200

Source. *The World's Car Manufacturers,* Edition 4

C Global car production

Region	Number of new cars sold
USA, Canada and Mexico	19 770 000
South America	1 922 000
Western Europe	15 120 000
Eastern Europe	2 592 000
Middle East	1 017 000
Africa	619 000
Japan	4 230 000
Asia except Japan	3 520 000
Australia/New Zealand	645 000
World	**49 435 000**

B New car sales, 2000

Global car production bar values:
- USA, Canada and Mexico: 17 384 000
- Western Europe: 15 397 000
- Eastern Europe: 2 703 000
- Asia except Japan: 4 803 000
- Middle East: 263 000
- Japan: 8 255 000
- South America: 1 665 000
- Africa: 228 000

E Demonstrations against the closure of the Longbridge plant in 2000

D Launch of the new Mini

F Using technology to make cars

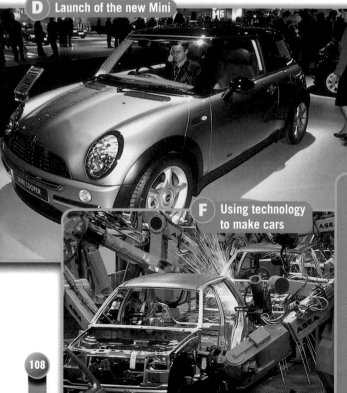

Learn about

In this unit you will learn about:

🌀 the global car industry

🌀 changes in the car industry in the UK

🌀 BMW, a global car producer

🌀 the car industry in Europe.

You will use the Internet to gain information on the car industry, to find out people's opinions on changes in the car industry, and as a way of communicating your findings and feelings to fellow pupils.

Activities

1 In pairs, discuss graph **A** and photographs **D–F.** What do they tell you about changes in the car industry? Share your ideas before making a list of the changes.

2 Use the data in table **B** to draw located bars showing new car sales on a world map. You will need a base outline map of the world. (123)

3 **a** Describe the pattern of global car production shown on map **C**.

  b Compare car production (map **C**) with the map you have drawn to show car sales.

  c Explain your findings. For example:
   - ⊚ suggest reasons why some regions have high or low sales
   - ⊚ suggest reasons why some regions make many or few cars.

Research activity (ICT)

4 Use the Internet to investigate the global car industry.

  a Visit the statistics section of the website for the UK auto industry using http://www.heinemann.co.uk/hotlinks.

  b Click on the World icon – How many cars were produced in total in 2000?

  c Now click on the Sales icon, then the World icon – How many sales were there in 1999?

  d Now decide on some questions of your own, to test a friend. This is a huge website so you have plenty of questions to choose from!

How to ...

... draw located bar charts

1 Map **C** shows you how to draw located bars. Make sure that each bar is located on or near the place it represents.

2 Use a similar scale for your map of car sales.

Try a scale of 2 mm = 1 million new cars sold.

help!

Good geographers look for key points when describing and explaining global patterns. Clever geographers make it sound easy! For example, consider:

- ✿ which regions are the largest producers?
- ✿ which regions are the less important producers?
- ✿ are most of the producers MEDCs or LEDCs?
- ✿ are they in the northern hemisphere (north of the Equator) or in the southern hemisphere (south of the Equator)?
- ✿ are there any exceptions?

Websites like this are always being updated; look out for the latest figures!

The UK car industry

A BMW's factory at Cowley, Oxford

Most car **manufacturers** look for a number of **factors** when they are building a new factory. These include:

- a large area of cheap, flat land
- good **communications** (road and rail links)
- a reliable and skilled workforce
- a nearby **market** for selling cars
- supporting industries that make **components** like tyres and glass.

The UK's car industry is very important to the country's economy. About 790 000 jobs depend on it, including about 330 000 workers directly employed in making vehicles and components. The UK has over twenty motor vehicle manufacturers, but six **multinational companies** produce almost three-quarters of all cars. They are:

- Ford (including Jaguar and Land Rover)
- Vauxhall (owned by General Motors)
- Peugeot
- Honda
- Nissan
- Toyota.

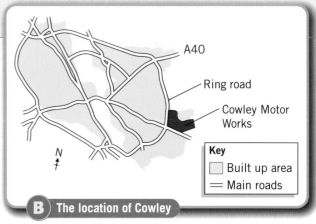

A40

Ring road

Cowley Motor Works

N

Key
- Built up area
- Main roads

B The location of Cowley

Changes in jobs

The car industry changes very quickly. Since the 1960s many UK car firms have been taken over by rival firms and some have gone out of business altogether. For example, in 2000 BMW sold Rover and Land Rover, and in 2001 Ford stopped producing the Escort at its Dagenham factory. These changes affect many people and other businesses. For example, the car works at Cowley in Oxford employed over 25 000 workers in the 1970s. By 2000 it employed just 2500 workers. But in 2001 production of the new Mini created more than 1000 extra jobs (photographs **A** and **C**).

Despite these changes, many companies still make cars and commercial vehicles in the UK. As shown on map **D**, many of them are specialist firms. As well as car manufacturers, over 1250 other companies make car components, and more than 100 000 people work in the car components industry, which makes £8 billion a year.

C The new Mini assembly line

Changes in car production

More and more new cars are being made and sold. In the UK in 1999:

- ⊚ new car registrations reached 2.2 million, the fourth highest figure on record
- ⊚ sales of cars were worth more than £31 billion
- ⊚ car production reached its highest level since 1972, but the manufacture of vans, lorries and coaches went down.

As well as changes in the number of cars produced, car manufacturers sell increasing numbers of cars abroad as **exports**. More than 1.1 million passenger cars were produced for export in 1999 – more than three times the exports in 1990.

Changes in investment

When car companies want to build a new car, they need to **invest** money in new designs, new equipment, and sometimes new factories. These are very expensive. Since the late 1970s Japanese and American car companies have invested huge sums of money in the European car industry, much of it in the UK. Since 1997, companies have invested over £3 billion in the UK car industry, creating approximately 9700 jobs.

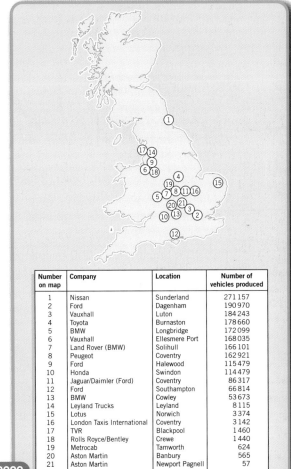

Number on map	Company	Location	Number of vehicles produced
1	Nissan	Sunderland	271 157
2	Ford	Dagenham	190 970
3	Vauxhall	Luton	184 243
4	Toyota	Burnaston	178 660
5	BMW	Longbridge	172 099
6	Vauxhall	Ellesmere Port	168 035
7	Land Rover (BMW)	Solihull	166 101
8	Peugeot	Coventry	162 921
9	Ford	Halewood	115 479
10	Honda	Swindon	114 479
11	Jaguar/Daimler (Ford)	Coventry	86 317
12	Ford	Southampton	66 814
13	BMW	Cowley	53 673
14	Leyland Trucks	Leyland	8 115
15	Lotus	Norwich	3 374
16	London Taxis International	Coventry	3 142
17	TVR	Blackpool	1 460
18	Rolls Royce/Bentley	Crewe	1 440
19	Metrocab	Tamworth	624
20	Aston Martin	Banbury	565
21	Aston Martin	Newport Pagnell	57

D UK car production in the UK, 2000

Activities

❶ Study photograph **A**, which shows the BMW factory at Cowley. Draw a sketch of the site and label the features that help describe and explain its location. Use the list of factors to help you.

❷ Use a large copy of map **D** to help you investigate the distribution of the UK car industry. ①②③

  a Use different colours to highlight:
- ⊚ small specialist factories (under 10 000 vehicles)
- ⊚ mass-production factories (over 100 000 vehicles)
- ⊚ medium-sized factories (10 000 – 100 000 vehicles).

  b Use symbols to identify the factories owned by multinational companies.

  c Add labels to your map, or write a short paragraph describing the distribution of car factories, then explain your findings.

❸ Study the data in map **D** and read the text again. Why is the closure of car factories so important to the local and the national economy? To help you with this, have a class discussion first. Ask your teacher to explain:

- ⊚ Jobs
- ⊚ Taxes
- ⊚ Knock-on jobs (the multiplier effect)
- ⊚ Imports / exports.

Research activity ⒾⒸⓉ

❹ The Internet is a useful way for geographers to collect data. It is easy to find information from a range of sources, including newspapers, governments, companies and pressure groups.

Remember: some information on the Internet is unreliable or wrong. It might be biased in favour of the people who produced it. Visit the statistics section of the website for the UK auto industry using www.heinemann.co.uk/hotlinks. Search for data on the world's largest vehicle manufacturers.

  a How many of the world's top ten largest manufacturers belong to the UK?

  b Which country has the most companies in the world's largest car companies?

  c What changes in UK car production can you identify?

Case Study
Cowley

Rover fact file

- 1904: First Rover car produced.
- 1994: Rover bought by BMW, who paid £800 million.
- Brands – Rover, Land Rover, Range Rover, Mini and MG.
- Main UK factories at Longbridge, Solihull, Cowley and Swindon.
- 1999: Employed 37 000 people, with 50 000 jobs at firms supplying Rover.
- 1999: UK sales ranked sixth behind Ford, Vauxhall, Peugeot, Renault and Volkswagen.
- 1994–2000: Rover lost £550 million, with sales down 45 per cent.
- 2000: BMW sold Rover, MG and Land Rover.
- 2001: Production of the new BMW Mini began at its Cowley factory.

Back to the future for Cowley

- BMW have helped to rebuild the Cowley factory with £230M.
- The workforce has been retrained.
- 100 000 Minis a year could be produced in the near future.

C This business park has been built on the former Cowley Works

BMW at Cowley

- The Cowley factory has been kept open and it uses more robots than ever before.
- Employment has gone down from 25 000 (1970) to 3 500 (2001).
- The size of the factory has been much reduced.
- Spare land has been snapped up for housing, shops and a business park.

See sources **A–E**.

A Extract from an OS map of the Cowley Works during its heyday, scale: 1:25 000

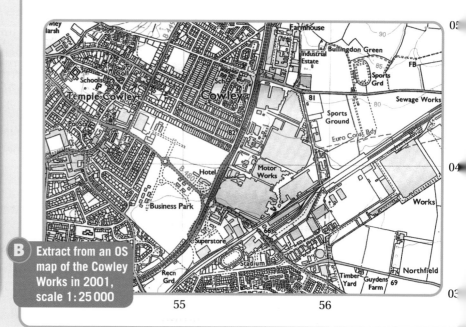

B Extract from an OS map of the Cowley Works in 2001, scale 1:25 000

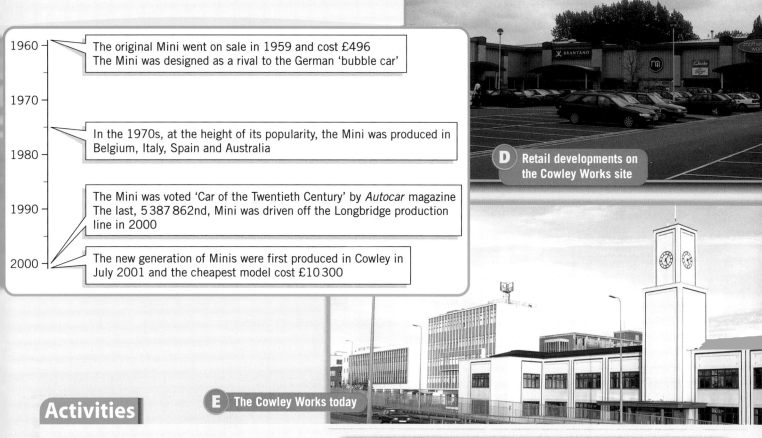

1960 — The original Mini went on sale in 1959 and cost £496
The Mini was designed as a rival to the German 'bubble car'

1970 —

1980 — In the 1970s, at the height of its popularity, the Mini was produced in Belgium, Italy, Spain and Australia

1990 — The Mini was voted 'Car of the Twentieth Century' by *Autocar* magazine
The last, 5 387 862nd, Mini was driven off the Longbridge production line in 2000

2000 — The new generation of Minis were first produced in Cowley in July 2001 and the cheapest model cost £10 300

D Retail developments on the Cowley Works site

E The Cowley Works today

Activities

1. Changes at the Cowley works have been good (positive) and bad (negative). Working in pairs, make a large copy of the diagram opposite and complete it. You can find evidence to help you on pages 112–3.

2. Two local people were asked about the changes. Which view do you agree with? Explain why.

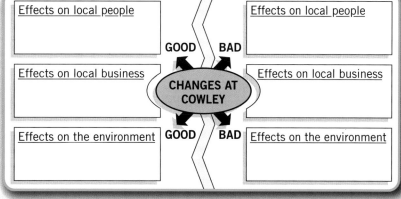

Effects on local people — GOOD — BAD — Effects on local people

Effects on local business — CHANGES AT COWLEY — Effects on local business

Effects on the environment — GOOD — BAD — Effects on the environment

Bring back the old days when 25 000 people worked here

I'd rather have new houses and shopping facilities here

Research activity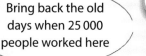

3. **a** Study an on-line map of the Oxford area from the Oxford City website through www.heinemann.co.uk/hotlinks.

   b Compare the information on this map with maps **A** and **B**. How useful is the online map? Give reasons.

   c Investigate and compare maps of Oxford from other websites such as Ordnance Survey or Map Blast! at www.heinemann.co.uk/hotlinks.

4. Investigate BMW's UK website using the Heinemann hotlinks address to see what you can find out about the Mini.

Case Study

BMW – a European and global car manufacturer

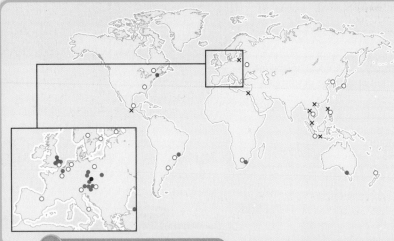

Key
- ● Munich Headquarters
- ● Production
- × Assembly plants
- ○ Sales and distribution locations

● **Production**
Berlin Plant
Birmingham Plant, UK
Dingolfing Plant
Eisenach Plant
Hams Hall Plant, UK
Landshut Plant
Munich Plant
Oxford Plant, UK
Regensburg Plant
Rosslyn Plant, South Africa
Spartanburg Plant, USA
Steyr Plant, Austria
Swindon Plant, UK
Tritec Motors Ltda, Curitiba, Brazil
Wackersdoft Plant

× **Assembly plants**
Toluca Plant, Mexico
Arnata City Plant, Thailand
CKD Production Cairo, Egypt
CKD Production Jakarta, Indonesia
CKD Production Kuala Lumpur, Malaysia
CKD Production Manila, Philippines
CKD Production Kaliningrad, Russia
CKD Production Hanoi, Vietnam

○ **Sales and distribution locations**

Argentina	Italy	Sweden
Australia	Japan	Switzerland
Austria	Mexico	Thailand
Belgium	New Zealand	USA
Brazil	Netherlands	
Canada	Norway	
Finland	Philippines	
France	Russia	
Germany	South Africa	
United Kingdom	South Korea	
Indonesia	Spain	

A BMW's global activities, 2000

The car industry in Europe is complex and fast-changing. There are many different car manufacturers – most of these have a number of factories, often in different countries. BMW, based in Germany, is one of these multinational companies. Like other car manufacturers:

- Big decisions are taken at the company's **head office** located in a large city. BMW's head office is in Munich.

- Car assembly factories put together large parts of cars which have been made somewhere else. They are often located where wages are low, e.g. in South-East Asia.

- Car production factories make whole cars from start to finish, so they are usually located in areas with a skilled workforce, e.g. BMW has production factories in Germany and Austria.

- Sales offices are usually located in cities where there are enough wealthy people to buy the cars.

B BMW's headquarters in Munich

C The production factory in Spartanburg, USA

BMW's success

BMW is a very successful company, which makes high-quality cars which are at the cutting edge of new technology. This image has helped its sales to increase every year. For example, in the USA General Motors and Ford sell many more vehicles, but BMW makes more than twice as much profit on each car it sells.

BMW is not alone in its success. In Germany as a whole the car industry grew in the 1990s. For example, 75 000 new jobs were created between 1998 and 1999 and over DM700 million (£200 million) was invested in the industry in the years between 1995 and 2000. German car factories make 35 per cent of all the cars made in the European Union and 14 per cent in the world.

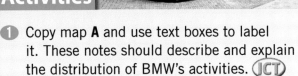

D One of BMW's sales offices

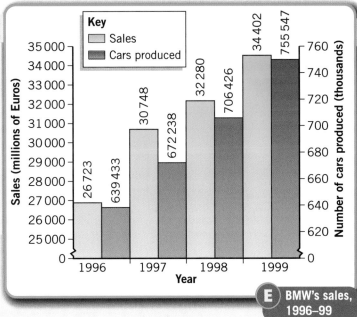

E BMW's sales, 1996–99

Activities

1 Copy map **A** and use text boxes to label it. These notes should describe and explain the distribution of BMW's activities. (ICT)

2 Study the information about BMW.

a With a partner, discuss the effects of BMW's success for people and businesses in Munich, and on the local environment. Remember there may be positive as well as negative effects.

b Make notes from your discussion using a copy of the table below to help you:

	Positive effects	Negative effects
On people		
On businesses		
On the environment		

c Write a short paragraph explaining who or what you think are the winners and losers from the changes at BMW.

Research activity (ICT)

3 a Investigate other car manufacturers in Europe by searching the Internet. You could work in groups, with each group investigating a different company.

b Find out the image of the company each website presents, and discuss what message it is trying to give to its customers.

c Find out what the site tells you about changes in the company.

d Compare the geographical information you have found out from each site – for example, where the company's activities are, and whether these are changing.

help!

You might like to think about people and places outside Germany too.

4 **Extension**

a Investigate BMW's environmental policies using its website through www.heinemann.co.uk/hotlinks. List the measures the company says it is taking to protect the environment.

b Find a website for an environmental pressure group, such as Friends of the Earth. Investigate their views on transport issues, and especially the effects of cars. List the key points.

c Compare the views of the car manufacturer and environmental groups, explaining any similarities and differences you have found.

Car production in Europe

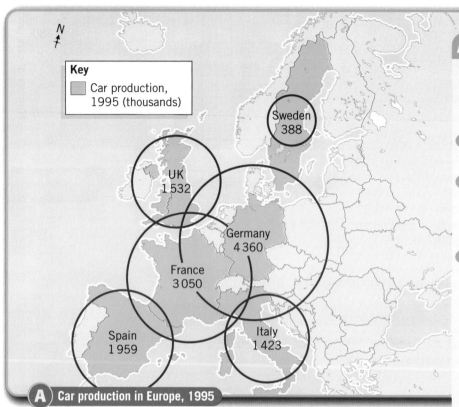

Key

Car production, 1995 (thousands)

Sweden 388

UK 1 532

Germany 4 360

France 3 050

Spain 1 959

Italy 1 423

A Car production in Europe, 1995

The market for cars in western Europe has grown from 13.4 million in 1997 to more than 15 million in 2000. At the same time, the market in North America has been booming. Wealthy consumers there buy many specialist European cars such as BMW, Mercedes and Porsche.

In spite of this, the car industry in western Europe is in crisis. A major problem is over-capacity. This means that car factories here are able to produce over 21 million cars a year, but in fact they sell only about 14.4 million cars a year. One solution is to cut costs by moving production to cheaper locations, for example Eastern Europe where wages are lower. Another is to join together with other companies. For example:

- Ford recently bought Land Rover and gained control of Volvo

- Daimler have merged with Chrysler and Mitsubishi.

Of course, these changes often have an impact on people, places and the environment near the car factories, as well as further away. Where there is economic change, there are usually winners and losers.

Activities

Map **A** shows car production in the mid 1990s. The research activity requires you to update it with current information.

1. Describe the pattern of car production as shown in map **A**.

2. Suggest reasons why some European countries produce more than others.

Research activity

3. As well as searching for information, geographers can collect information from the Internet and present it in a variety of forms, using word processing or spreadsheets for example. But good geographers never copy direct – they always select information and adapt it to make it their own work.

   a Use the Internet to investigate car production in Europe, using one of these websites through www.heinemann.co.uk/hotlinks:
   - UK Auto Industry statistics page, or
   - German Verband de Automobilindustrie

   b Find out about changing car production in Europe, using these headings to help you:
   - the main car-producing countries
   - changes in car production in the past 5–10 years
   - the main car-manufacturing companies.

   c You could present your data by:
   - copying information into a spreadsheet then using the program to sort the data and present it as charts
   - selecting useful text, copying it into a word processor, then editing it by using bullets and subheadings, and highlighting key points
   - using a presentation program to present your findings and your conclusions about change.

Review and reflect

Activities

1 You are familiar with finding answers to questions, especially geographical questions like the Six Ws: **W**hat? **W**here? **W**ho? **W**hen? **W**hy? Ho**W**? In pairs, look back over this unit and work out suitable questions to go with the answers below.

   a 58.2 million.

   b Car components.

   c Workers and other businesses at Cowley.

   d Mainly in Europe and North America.

   e Wages are lower there, so companies can make better profits.

   f General Motors.

   g A skilled workforce.

   h Robots do many tasks in the factory.

help!

Remember some questions have only one answer, others can have several.

2 **a** Work out between five and ten of your own answers on the theme of the changing car industry. Try to make sure you have at least one for each of the Six Ws.

   b Test a partner to see if they can work out the questions to go with your answers.

3 Write a short report on the changing car industry and its effects, using the Six Ws to help you write headings. If you use a word processing or presentation program to present your report, you could include hyperlinks to the most useful websites you have used in this unit. **ICT**

A What next?

8 Local actions, global effects

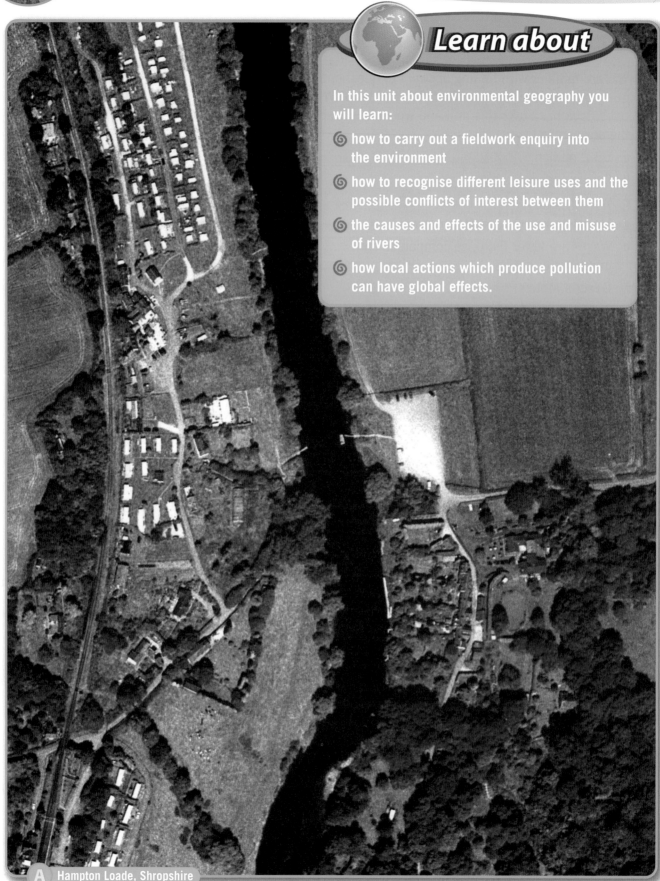

Learn about

In this unit about environmental geography you will learn:

- how to carry out a fieldwork enquiry into the environment
- how to recognise different leisure uses and the possible conflicts of interest between them
- the causes and effects of the use and misuse of rivers
- how local actions which produce pollution can have global effects.

A Hampton Loade, Shropshire

Fieldwork enquiry

A class of students were doing some geographical fieldwork by a river. Each student was expected to focus their investigation on one of these questions, although they were encouraged to ask further questions as their fieldwork progressed.

- How has the settlement changed over the years?
- What land use is found on and by this stretch of river?
- How could the tourist industry in the area grow?
- What visitor pressures are there on the settlement?
- What conflicts occur as a result of the land use in this area?

The next four pages show how one student went about his enquiry. You will be asked to decide which enquiry question he chose, from the list above.

First of all, Edward got the most detailed map that he could find. He tried the Environment Agency (use the links at www.heinemann.co.uk/hotlinks).

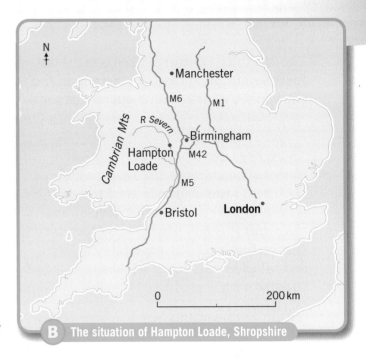

B The situation of Hampton Loade, Shropshire

C Introducing Edward

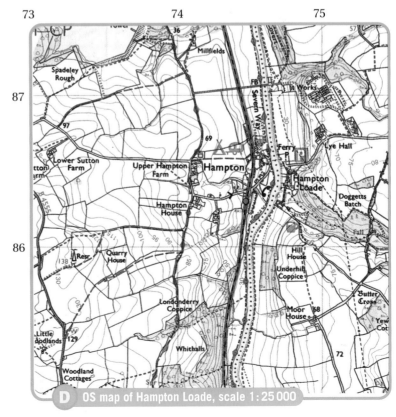

D OS map of Hampton Loade, scale 1:25 000

Local actions: profile of a ferryman

The first thing Edward noticed was the last surviving rope ferry on the River Severn. He spoke to the ferryman and took some photographs; you can see what he found out on this page.

There has been a passenger ferry at Hampton Loade since the seventeenth century. It was originally used to ferry miners to work on the other side of the river, but it is now used only by tourists. Darren took over the rope ferry in 1996, and relies on hot, sunny weekends in order to make a small profit.

E | **The rope ferry at Hampton Loade**

F | **How the rope ferry works**

River current

N
W ← → E
S

Rope across river

LS

F

Ferry moves

Rudder

LS

Car park

Key
F Ferry
LS Landing stage

I live in a small caravan on the western side of the Severn. When a passenger wants to go across the river, they ring a bell and I appear! The ferry is unlocked from its mooring and by moving the rudder I can use the current of the river to move the boat across to the over side.

I can see that one day I may be forced to give up, and that will be another piece of English heritage lost forever.

If the weather is poor, no one visits the area at all. Many of my passengers come by the Severn Valley Railway – there's a beautiful little station 200 metres up the hill. If that's not running, I might as well not bother! People also stay at home if there's a big sporting event on the television.

G | **Darren the ferryman**

I can't really go away during the summer, because if I don't offer the service, people won't come back. During the winter, however, I have to be very aware of the water level. Last winter's flooding was a nightmare. Both the landing stages that people use to get onto the ferry were destroyed by debris, including uprooted trees, that the flood water brought down from upstream. They can cost £1000 each to replace.

If I can't get funds from another source, I feel it's just a matter of time before I go broke!

What leisure activities are located on and by the river?

Edward discovered from a noticeboard that Hampton Loade is a small settlement on the banks of the River Severn in Shropshire. It is now a peaceful riverside scene, but 150 years ago it was very industrial, with mills and forges nearby making paper, flour and iron.

The settlement has houses on both sides of the river. On the eastern side there is a pub, a restaurant and one or two houses. The western side contains more buildings, including a railway station on the Severn Valley Railway, which often runs steam locomotives.

Edward made field sketch **H** of the settlement during a visit in late August.

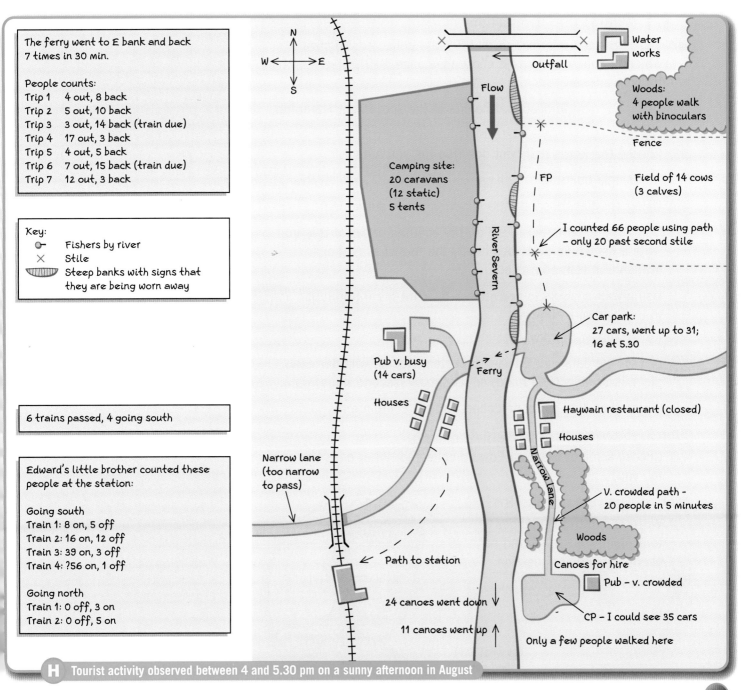

H Tourist activity observed between 4 and 5.30 pm on a sunny afternoon in August

Writing up the fieldwork enquiry

The students were told to write up their field enquiry in four parts:

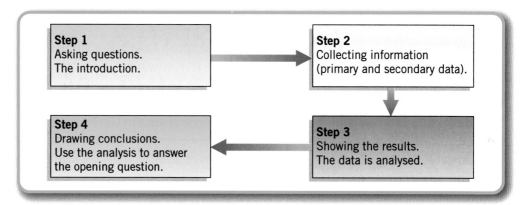

Step 1
Asking questions.
The introduction.

Step 2
Collecting information
(primary and secondary data).

Step 3
Showing the results.
The data is analysed.

Step 4
Drawing conclusions.
Use the analysis to answer
the opening question.

Activities

Step 1 – Writing the introduction

1 Looking at the information that Edward collected, suggest which enquiry question he chose (see page 119). Give reasons for your answer.

2 Using OS map **D**, describe the *site* of the settlement Hampton Loade.

3 Choose the words that best describe the settlement:

   single building   village   sub-town   market town.

4 Using an atlas, describe the *situation* of the settlement.

5 Using the information found on the opening pages of this unit, write a list which describes briefly the tourist attractions available in Hampton Loade.

6 Using your answers to activities **1–5**, write the introduction to the fieldwork enquiry.

Step 2 – Collecting the data

7 List all the data that Edward collected. Decide whether each piece is *primary* (first hand) or *secondary* (second hand) data.

8 What other data could he collect to help complete his work?

Step 3 – Showing the results (data analysis)

9 Choose some of the data Edward collected. What does the data tell you?

Step 4 – Drawing conclusions

10 Write one or two sentences to explain what *you* found out about the enquiry question.

help!

What was the enquiry question?
Where was the fieldwork carried out?

help!

- Use aerial photograph **A** and OS extract **C** to improve the sketch map, which should appear in the middle of your display.

- Your teacher will give you advice about changing the data into graphs and sketches.

- When choosing the data make sure that you link it back to the enquiry question chosen in **1**.

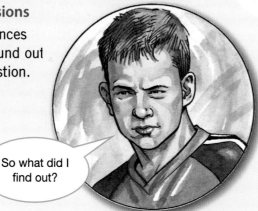

So what did I find out?

What conflicts can occur between recreational activities ?

Geographers sometimes call places like Hampton Loade **honeypot sites**.
Such sites attract great numbers of visitors, especially in the summer season,
at weekends, and during fine weather.

A The competing demands of recreation in Hampton Loade

B Tourism – for and against

The good points

- Tourism brings money and jobs to areas which otherwise would have little local employment.

- Money from tourism can be used to improve local infrastructure, such as utilities (gas, electricity supply, mains drainage), television reception and mobile phone coverage. Better roads and facilities like shops, public transport and street lighting benefit local people.

The not-so-good points

- Honeypot sites can get so busy that some controls are needed. If these areas are not carefully controlled, the things that people come to visit may become spoilt and the area will not be visited anymore.

- The tourist season is very short, especially in Britain where the weather is unreliable, so that many of the jobs only last for part of the year.

- Many of the jobs created by the tourist industry are neither highly skilled nor well paid.

The conflicts

When people visit an area, they usually choose a particular activity. The variety of recreational activities on offer at Hampton Loade is excellent for attracting visitors. Unfortunately, there can be some conflict between activities.

Activities

1 a Use the labels around photograph **A** to make a list of some leisure activities in Hampton Loade.

b Add any other leisure uses that you can think of to your list. You may find OS map **D** on page 119, sketch map **H** on page 121 and other information in this unit useful.

2 Write a short description of the ideal conditions for each of the leisure users you have listed.

3 Use your answer to question **2** to help you complete a conflict matrix to show how each leisure activity might conflict with other recreational activities. The matrix has been started for you.

4 In a class discussion, try to agree which activities should be controlled because they cause conflict.

	Fishing	**Walking**	**Canoeing**
Fishing		✗	
Walking	0		
Canoeing			

Key: ✗ = some conflict
✗✗ = great conflict
0 = no conflict
? = difficult to decide

Managing leisure activities to reduce conflict

Conflicts may be overcome in a number of ways.

© **Power:** Those activities which are more powerful may 'win the day' because they are either not regulated or earn more money. Recreational activity has to put up with it or disappear.

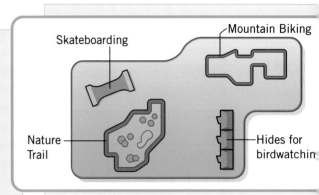

Skateboarding
Mountain Biking
Nature Trail
Hides for birdwatching

© **Zoning:** Different activities can be given different areas in which to operate, so that conflicts are kept to a minimum.

© **Time solutions:** Conflicts can be reduced by allowing recreational users to operate at different times of the day or year.

Skateboarders banned from park – council plan purpose-built ramps

© **Buying off:** The losers in a conflict may be given some form of compensation to make up for their loss. For example, they may be given somewhere else to use.

© **Lessen the bad effects:** The activities of the 'winners' in a conflict are controlled so as to minimise their bad effects.

Visitor Centre

Activities

⑤ Suggest how each of the following decisions might affect the lives of the residents and other leisure users in the Hampton Loade area.

  a Allowing loud music to be broadcast from one of the pubs.

  b Allowing small power boats on the stretch of river.

  c Closing down the public car park.

  d Stopping people using the footpaths in the area.

  e Replacing cattle with intensive crops.

⑥ On the basis of your answers to **5,** put the five decisions in order of the environmental effect they might have. Write brief reasons for your answer.

⑦ Think of a leisure conflict in your own area. Have a class discussion and argue how the conflict could be reduced.

help!

Try to think of the effects that might result from these decisions and how they might affect the activities of other people.

How do people use and misuse rivers?
Case Study

Rhine River Basin and fresh water pollution

The River Rhine is one of the world's busiest rivers. It flows through many important countries in the heartland of Europe: from the Swiss mountains the Rhine's course goes past and into the Bodensee. From there its course marks first the Swiss-German border and then the French-German border. It finally flows through Germany and into the Netherlands. The Rhine basin is very densely populated as a result of highly developed industry, trade and agriculture, as well as a dense network of motorways and railways. Demands on the river have therefore been very heavy. Although the Rhine is much cleaner than it used to be, pollution from manufacturing industry, from farming and from sewage remains a major international problem.

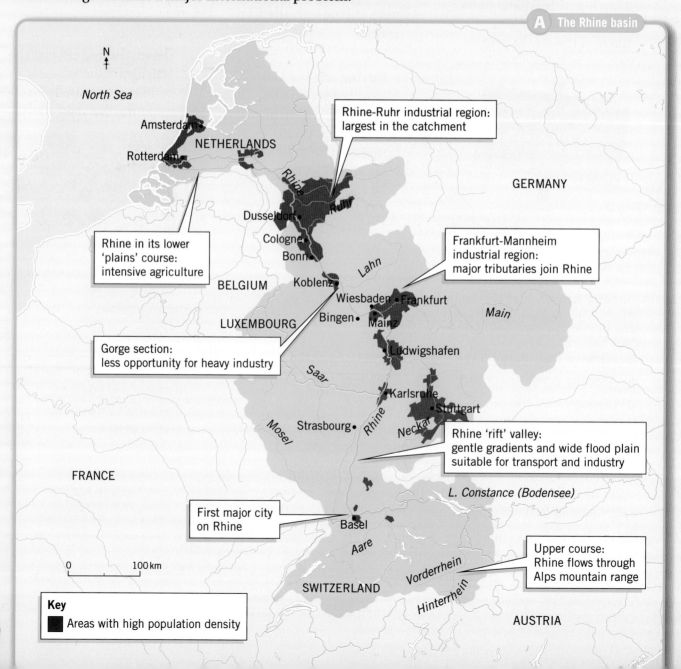

A The Rhine basin

Rhine-Ruhr industrial region: largest in the catchment

Rhine in its lower 'plains' course: intensive agriculture

Frankfurt-Mannheim industrial region: major tributaries join Rhine

Gorge section: less opportunity for heavy industry

Rhine 'rift' valley: gentle gradients and wide flood plain suitable for transport and industry

First major city on Rhine

Upper course: Rhine flows through Alps mountain range

North Sea · Amsterdam · NETHERLANDS · Rotterdam · Rhine · Ruhr · GERMANY · Dusseldorf · Cologne · Bonn · Lahn · BELGIUM · Koblenz · Wiesbaden · Frankfurt · Main · LUXEMBOURG · Bingen · Mainz · Ludwigshafen · Saar · Karlsruhe · Stuttgart · Mosel · Strasbourg · Rhine · Neckar · L. Constance (Bodensee) · FRANCE · Basel · Aare · Vorderrhein · SWITZERLAND · Hinterrhein · AUSTRIA

0   100 km

Key
■ Areas with high population density

B Sources of pollution on the River Rhine

Key
- 🌀 Chemicals
- 🌀 Oil refining
- 🌀 Thermal power station

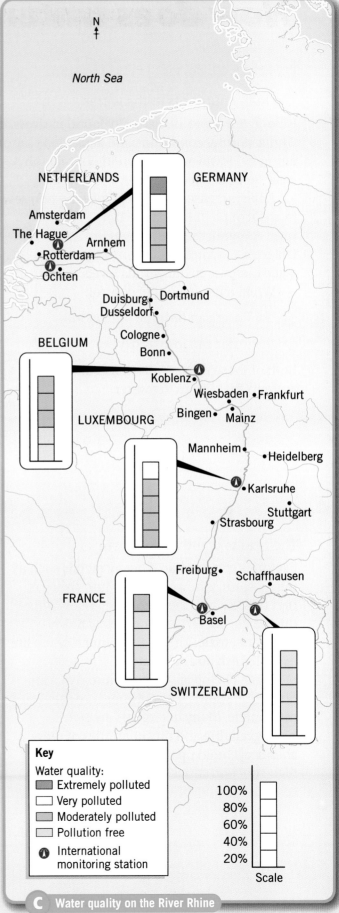

C Water quality on the River Rhine

Key
Water quality:
- ▨ Extremely polluted
- ☐ Very polluted
- ▨ Moderately polluted
- ▨ Pollution free
- 🜛 International monitoring station

100%
80%
60%
40%
20%

Scale

How does water become polluted?

Fresh water pollution

Too many nutrients in the water

Blue-green algae are naturally found in rivers and lakes. Under normal conditions, the algae don't harm fish or animals. However, as shown in photograph **A**, things can easily get out of control.

A big increase in algae can occur when sewage and waste from farming or industry enters a river. Ask your teacher to explain Diagram **B**, which shows you why the algae increase to dangerous levels.

When algae get out of control:

- the water can become poisonous.

- the water can lose its oxygen.

Both of these things will kill fish and animals that live in the water.

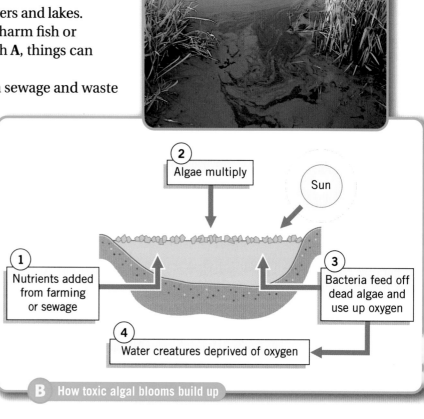

A Green scum appears on the surface of a lake

2 Algae multiply

Sun

1 Nutrients added from farming or sewage

3 Bacteria feed off dead algae and use up oxygen

4 Water creatures deprived of oxygen

B How toxic algal blooms build up

The results of industrial waste

Factories can discharge heavy metals such as magnesium, zinc and copper into rivers as part of the waste they produce. Rivers *dilute* this waste, but large quantities of heavy metals are toxic. They poison much of the life in both fresh and salt water.

Some chemicals dumped into rivers are not broken down naturally because they are man-made. Many detergents are not **biodegradable** and tiny quantities of these chemicals build up in animals over time. In high concentrations they can kill.

Rainwater

Falling rain may contain some harmful chemicals released into the air by factories and by vehicles. Rainwater that runs off fields, which are treated with pesticides or fertilisers, carries the chemicals into rivers. Rain landing on roads can take oil or **particulates** from car exhausts into the drains and eventually into rivers.

C Oil and particulates from vehicles drain eventually into rivers

Birds suffer from oil pollution in three ways. It kills their food, and also clogs their feathers so they are no longer waterproof and the birds get cold. When the birds try to clean themselves, they are poisoned by the oil.

Thermal pollution

Factories often use water from rivers for cooling. When the water is returned to the river it is warmer, and this can have environmental impacts. Some helpful bacteria may be killed by just slight increases in temperature. This is called **thermal pollution**.

E A coal-fired power station

An oiled sea-bird

D An oiled sea-bird

Indicators of pollution

Fish swimming through a river may not be much affected by pollution. But creatures that live on the bed of a river can show pollution levels very well. If conditions are wrong they cannot simply swim away. So these are sometimes called **indicator species**.

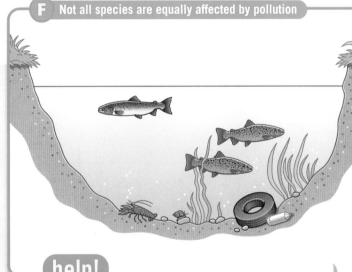

F Not all species are equally affected by pollution

Activities

1. Make a word bank of key words for this unit. Start with the words in bold on this page. Add any key words you have learned from pages 118–128.

2. Salmon need to travel up river to spawn (lay eggs). They must find a place with good quality, shallow water and a river bed made up of *gravel*, not *silt*. Imagine that you are a salmon making your way up the River Rhine from the sea. Describe your journey, noting any changes in water quality that you come across – try to explain these pollution events. Looking up the international IKSR website through www.heinemann.co.uk/hotlinks might help you. (ICT)

3. Pollution is headline news; write a newspaper article like the one opposite.

   a Choose *one* form of pollution from this section of work. Write a headline to report a major pollution problem.

   b Write the first part of your article to describe what has happened.

   c Then explain why the fish have died, based on the information you have learned from these pages.

   You could use a program such as Microsoft® Publisher to produce this piece of work. (ICT)

help!

Choose from: forestry, reservoir, sheep and dairy farming, light and hi-tech industry, power station, sewage works downstream of major settlement, intensive agriculture, industry from the Ruhr valley, pollution from motorway, dairy farming on the lower Rhine plain.

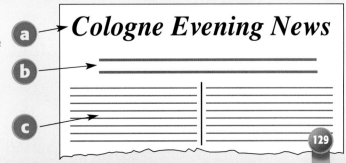

Cologne Evening News

'Behold the sea, the teeming sea ...'

Most river water, and any pollution that it carries, ends up in the sea. The sea has always been used as a dumping ground. In the past, people thought the world's oceans were so vast they could absorb any pollution they received. Today some seas are at serious risk from pollution: one example is the North Sea.

Seawater food chains

A Plankton are tiny, single-celled plants which float around in the top layer of the sea – they form the heart of the food web

B There may be many millions of copepods in each cubic metre of water – these graze off the phytoplankton

C Floating in the sea's currents, jellyfish trap copepods and anything else that swims against their long trailing tentacles

D Starfish and sea-urchins feed on a wide variety of shellfish – they are 'keystone' species that control the populations of some species

F Great grey seals eat a wide variety of fish, crustaceans and sea-urchins

E Herring and mackerel are surface fish which form shoals for safety from predators

G Killer whales feed on large fish, dolphins, seals and even other whales, but they are not known to attack humans

H About 90 000 gannets come to the North Sea to breed. They enjoy a diet of larger fish

The North Sea is one of the world's largest coastal seas but it only contains 1 per cent of the Earth's sea water. It is almost entirely surrounded by land, with the southern part narrowing to a **strait** of water 35 kilometres wide between Dover and Calais. As it is on the **continental shelf**, it is a mainly shallow sea between 25 and 55 metres deep. In the north, the Norwegian Trench is over 200 metres deep.

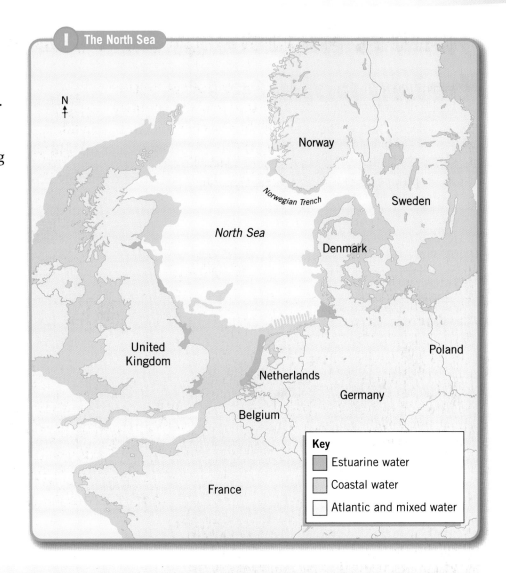

I **The North Sea**

Key
- Estuarine water
- Coastal water
- Atlantic and mixed water

Activities

1. Write a short paragraph to introduce the North Sea. Include information on its location and the scale of the area, as well as an outline of the Sea's physical and human geography.

2. Using the photographs on the opposite page, construct a food web diagram to show the feeding levels in the North Sea. Start by copying the diagram on the right.

3. **Extension**

   Navigate the website for Ball State University's exploring ecosystems to extend your web diagram at: www.heinemann.co.uk/hotlinks. (ICT)

4. Why is the North Sea so at risk from pollution? Use the information on this page, including map **J**, to help you.

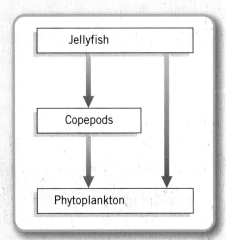

How is the North Sea being polluted?

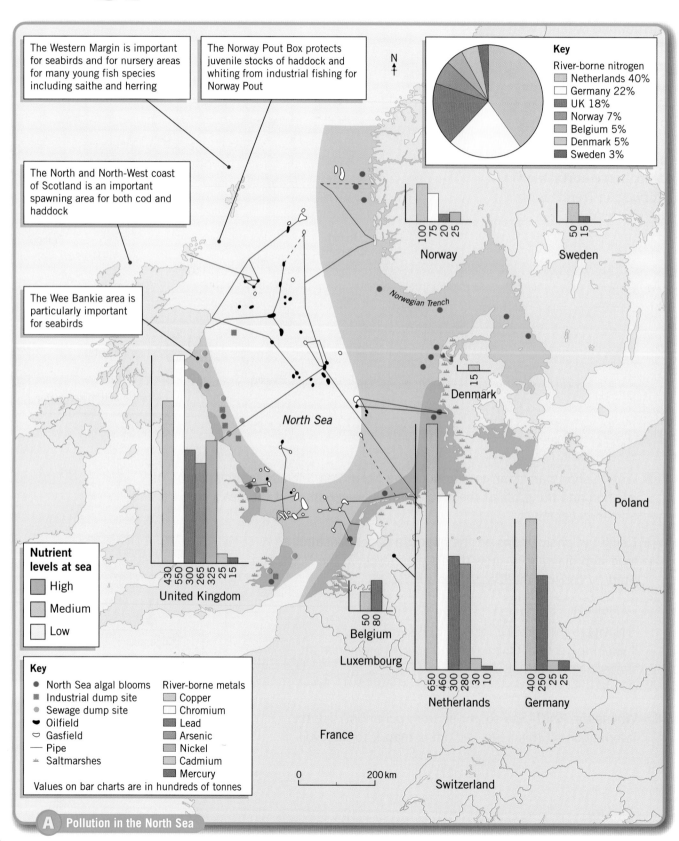

The Western Margin is important for seabirds and for nursery areas for many young fish species including saithe and herring

The Norway Pout Box protects juvenile stocks of haddock and whiting from industrial fishing for Norway Pout

The North and North-West coast of Scotland is an important spawning area for both cod and haddock

The Wee Bankie area is particularly important for seabirds

Key
River-borne nitrogen
- Netherlands 40%
- Germany 22%
- UK 18%
- Norway 7%
- Belgium 5%
- Denmark 5%
- Sweden 3%

N

Norway
100 75 20 25

Sweden
50 15

Norwegian Trench

North Sea

Denmark
15

Poland

Nutrient levels at sea
- High
- Medium
- Low

United Kingdom
430 550 300 265 325 25 15

Belgium
50 80

Luxembourg

Netherlands
650 460 300 280 30 10

Germany
400 250 25 25

France

Key
- North Sea algal blooms
- Industrial dump site
- Sewage dump site
- Oilfield
- Gasfield
- Pipe
- Saltmarshes

River-borne metals
- Copper
- Chromium
- Lead
- Arsenic
- Nickel
- Cadmium
- Mercury

Values on bar charts are in hundreds of tonnes

0   200 km

Switzerland

A Pollution in the North Sea

Europe's dustbin!

Over 50 million people live close to the shores of the North Sea. It is surrounded by some of the world's most industrialised nations. There is very great stress on the North Sea as it is **exploited** for a number of conflicting uses. Some are given below:

 intensive use of fish stocks for food

 as an important shipping route

 extraction of water to cool power stations

 as an area for relaxation

 extraction of sand and gravel for the building industry

 as a huge dump for the unwanted rubbish produced by advanced industrial nations.

 extraction of natural gas and oil

The pattern of currents means that it often takes three years for any waste to circulate back into the Atlantic Ocean. The North Sea has become one of the dirtiest and most polluted seas in the world.

Activities

1 Using map **A**, list all the causes of North Sea pollution. Try to name the country that is the chief polluter for each cause that you list.

2 Try to explain why the Netherlands appears to be adding the most river-borne heavy metals into the North Sea.

3 Explain how the sources of pollution that you have listed could affect each of the creatures mentioned on page 130. Put the creatures in order of danger and explain your decisions.

4 Explain at least two effects on the North Sea environment that would result from each of these measures.

   a An international ban on dumping rubbish at sea.

   b Making companies clean their waste products before they are put into rivers.

   c Heavy taxes on oil companies who pollute the sea.

   d Giving each country a strict quota (limit) on the amount of fish that can be caught.

5 In a class discussion:

   a Suggest what else could be done to reduce pollution.

   b Discuss why it will be difficult to reduce pollution in this 'international' sea.

Global effects

What is the future of Antarctica?

Activities

You are going to use the information on pages 134–139 to conduct a full enquiry using secondary sources. Your enquiry will be divided into the familiar sections:

- **Step 1: asking questions** – some questions have been suggested on this page. Try to break down your main question into smaller questions to help you plan out your work. The introduction should include background information including the location of the area; you will find suitable material on page 135.

- **Step 2: collecting information** – this section will include secondary data, which you can find on pages 136 – 139. You can find more secondary information by conducting a web enquiry using a search engine.

- **Step 3: showing the results** – the data is analysed in this section. You will have a great deal of information on Antarctica – pick out only the relevant parts.

- **Step 4: drawing conclusions** – at this point you draw the enquiry to a close by answering the opening enquiry question based upon your analysis.

How can Antarctica be conserved and managed to sustain its environment?

Why is Antarctica a fragile environment?

Why is Antarctica under threat?

How have the activities of the industrialised nations affected Antarctica?

Which parts of Antarctica are threatened with most damage?

A

Antarctica: the last wilderness

The very harsh and difficult environment of Antarctica means that the continent is not threatened by development which is causing problems in other places in the world. It is, however, a very fragile environment for a number of reasons.

- Nature works very slowly because of the intense cold. Dead creatures decay very slowly (see **C**).

- Food webs in this area depend upon one or two key species (see **D**).

- Conditions are so harsh that animals can breed successfully only in one or two areas; these areas are densely populated with animals and have unique ecosystems.

Fact file: Antarctica

- Antarctica has a climate which is drier than the Sahara Desert. Annual precipitation on the central plateau is only 300 mm in some places.

- Ninety-nine per cent of Antarctica is covered by a layer of ice thought to be 2500 metres thick. This makes the surface, on average, higher than that of any other continent.

- It is surrounded by the Southern Ocean, which is the most exposed and stormiest in the world.

- Antarctica is the windiest continent, as well as being extremely cold.

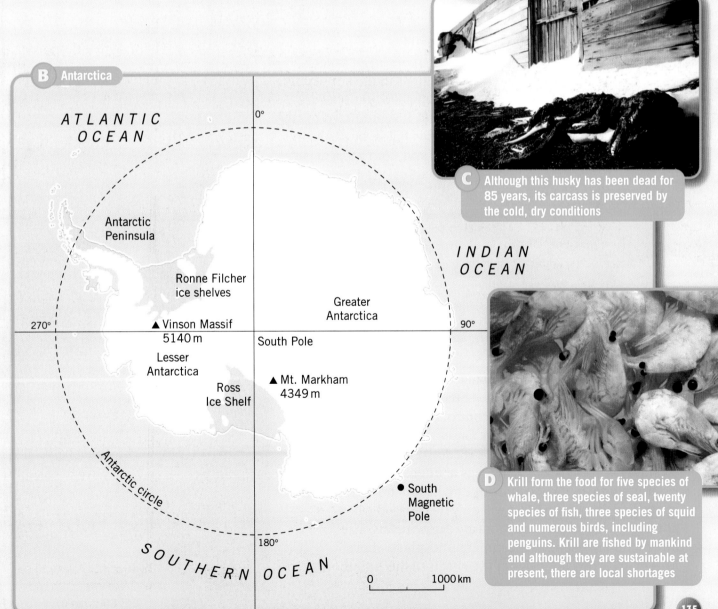

C Although this husky has been dead for 85 years, its carcass is preserved by the cold, dry conditions

B Antarctica

ATLANTIC OCEAN

0°

Antarctic Peninsula

Ronne Filcher ice shelves

INDIAN OCEAN

Greater Antarctica

270°

▲ Vinson Massif 5140 m

South Pole

90°

Lesser Antarctica

Ross Ice Shelf

▲ Mt. Markham 4349 m

Antarctic circle

● South Magnetic Pole

180°

SOUTHERN OCEAN

0   1000 km

D Krill form the food for five species of whale, three species of seal, twenty species of fish, three species of squid and numerous birds, including penguins. Krill are fished by mankind and although they are sustainable at present, there are local shortages

How does global air pollution affect Antarctica?

The issue of carbon dioxide (CO₂)

Greenhouse gases (GHGs) in the atmosphere allow the Sun's rays in but trap radiated heat from the Earth. **Carbon dioxide** is a gas that occurs naturally and helps to control the Earth's temperature. However, over the past 200 years the burning of coal and oil has increased the amount of carbon dioxide in the atmosphere. This has led to global warming by the **accelerated greenhouse effect**. A warmer atmosphere is likely to melt parts of the Antarctic ice cap. This could have global effects on sea levels and on ocean currents.

E Burning fossil fuels releases CO₂ into the atmosphere

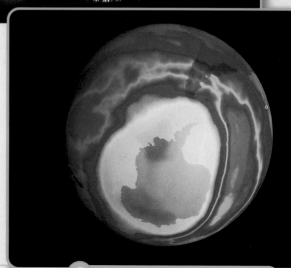

F Herds of cattle release CH₄ into the atmosphere

All about methane

Methane (CH₄) occurs in much smaller quantities in the atmosphere than carbon dioxide, but is a very powerful GHG. It is produced by rice grown in paddy fields, by cattle, in rubbish tips, and from other sources.

CFCs and the ozone problem

Ozone (O₃) is a poisonous substance which causes harmful pollution at ground level. On the other hand, ozone in the upper atmosphere, is vital for controlling the amount of incoming ultra-violet radiation. Gases like **chlorofluorocarbons (CFCs)** break down this protective shield. This effect is worse in areas of intense cold, especially in springtime. In most countries CFC production is strictly controlled, but many CFCs will only be released when appliances like old refrigerators are thrown away. The destruction of ozone in the upper atmosphere above Antarctica is one indicator of the effects of this pollution.

G False colour satellite image shows ozone 'hole' over the Antarctic

NOx and SOx

Sulphur dioxide (SO_2) and nitrogen oxides (NOx) are given off by coal-fired power stations and car exhausts. They reach the ground by rainfall or by dry deposition. Their effect is often felt further away as chimney stacks are now built increasingly high. They cause **acid rain**, which not only kills trees but causes streams and lakes to become 'dead' and lifeless.

H Pollution from vehicle exhausts can become locked into ice sheets

Lead and other heavy metals

Lead and other heavy metals are often found in vehicle exhausts and in the smoke released by factories. They can become trapped in the polar ice sheets. In Antarctica there are traces of heavy metals and organic toxins, which have been carried from the inhabited parts of the world. These will be returned to the environment if the ice melts.

I Acid rain can kill trees

J Dead lakes often look very beautiful but their clear water often means a lack of biological activity

Is the Antarctic ice sheet getting thinner?

Massive iceberg peels away from Antarctic ice shelf

A monster iceberg called B-15, 290 km long by 30 km wide, has broken away from Antarctica's Ross Ice Shelf. At 11 000 square kilometres in area, it is about half the size of Wales and looms 50 metres (fifteen storeys) above the water. Although very large icebergs occasionally calve from ice sheets, this one is thought to be the largest one ever.

K News report, March 2000

L Ice breaking away from the ice shelf

> We have been able to see cracks in the Antarctic ice shelf for many years. When large chunks of ice break off it is quite natural.

> Recently, the chunks of ice breaking away from the Antarctic ice shelf are getting bigger. Global warming is the cause.

> The result will be sea level rise as the icebergs melt. Th world's climate will also change; t will give us serious problems in the future.

M Two views on the Antarctic ice sheet

The loss of ice shelves from Antarctica

Are the large cracks which have appeared in the ice sheets around Antarctica part of a natural process or an effect of global warming? The *causes* are not certain. Some scientists believe that the *effects* of enormous quantities of ice melting in the Southern Ocean will change our climate. No one today can predict what will happen exactly, but these suggestions have been made:

- The Ross and Ronne ice shelves are like two big plugs which support the ice on the main part of Antarctica. If they melt the whole of the sheet will become unstable.

- The melting of ice shelves, made up of floating ice, will have no effect on world sea levels. However, if lots of cold water is suddenly released into the oceans, this may affect the pattern of ocean currents.

- Ocean currents are important in transferring heat from the Equator to the Poles. They stop the world overheating.

- Most of Antarctica has had a stable climate for the past 40 years. It is only the Antarctic peninsula that is warming at a rate of two to three times the global average.

- If there is less ice on the Poles, then fewer of the Sun's rays will be reflected back into space.

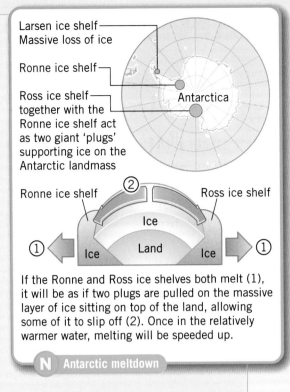

Larsen ice shelf — Massive loss of ice

Ronne ice shelf

Ross ice shelf together with the Ronne ice shelf act as two giant 'plugs' supporting ice on the Antarctic landmass

Ronne ice shelf — Ross ice shelf

If the Ronne and Ross ice shelves both melt (1), it will be as if two plugs are pulled on the massive layer of ice sitting on top of the land, allowing some of it to slip off (2). Once in the relatively warmer water, melting will be speeded up.

N Antarctic meltdown

Other stresses on the environment

Mining

Mining in Antarctica has been banned for at least the next 50 years through an international agreement called the Protocol on Environmental Protection to the Antarctic Treaty. There are, however, many valuable deposits of iron, oil and gas. In the future, when these minerals run out in other parts of the world, the pressure for mining here will become very strong.

Tourism

Increasingly Antarctic cruises are being offered to tourists who are keen to enjoy the wonders of the continent. There are fears that tourists will cause pressure on the fragile vegetation and disturb the breeding grounds of animals.

Impact of scientists

There are only ever about 10 000 scientists on an area 58 times the size of Britain. All rubbish and waste must be removed from the continent, and it is very expensive to dispose of. In such cold temperatures, the normal natural processes of decomposition are very slow.

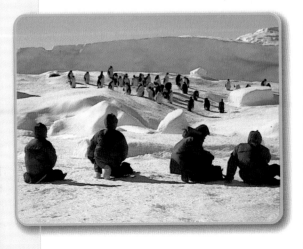

Review and reflect

What future is there for the ferryman at Hampton Loade?

Possible scenario 1: Business as usual!

Without agreements between land users, uncontrolled economic development could produce great advantages for a few in the short term. In the long term, it could bring disaster.

A

Possible scenario 2: Stop and think!

Agreement on stopping global warming might mean unpopular controls, including some on leisure activities. This course of action could provide a better long-term future for all developments.

B

Activities

1 Update your word bank so that it covers the whole unit. This will help you with the final activities. 📖

2 Read the headlines below. For each headline:

a Suggest whether the change is local, regional or global in scale.

b Explain what might have caused the change to happen and suggest what effects it might produce.

c Suggest how each change would affect the ferryman. Give your reasons.

> **help!**
>
> Think of all the possibilities – some might be good but some might be bad.

Ozone hole over the Arctic bigger than ever

North Sea fishermen forced to catch smaller fish

Global temperatures rise and rise!

Global warming brings more storms to Britain

Cheap fuel for the British motorist: fuel protestors triumphant!

The Arctic Ocean becomes a major shipping route

Maldive Islands finally disappear under the Indian Ocean

Overharvesting endangers krill supplies

European governments agree to control dirty factories

Breakthrough! Cheap and practical electric car available soon

3 Look carefully at cartoons **A** and **B**. They show two very different ideas of what might happen in Hampton Loade in the future.

a Describe each cartoon and say how they each give a very different idea about the future.

b Try to explain why the two cartoonists have different views of the future.

c In your own view, which is the more likely to happen? Give reasons for your viewpoint.

Glossary

Accelerated greenhouse effect   The increased warming of the Earth caused by humans burning fossil fuels. This leads to a build-up of carbon dioxide in the atmosphere, so less heat escapes into space.

Acid rain   Rain that contains dilute sulphuric or nitric acid. The acids come from air pollution and are dissolved by the rain as it falls to earth.

Active zone   An area where two tectonic plates meet. Earthquakes and volcanoes occur in active zones.

Biodegradable   Able to be broken down naturally and harmlessly, for example by bacteria.

Blue-green algae   Algae are small, simple plants that live in water. Blue–green algae increase rapidly in water which is rich in nutrients, especially in strong sunlight.

Caldera complexes   A type of volcano which has exploded in the past, forming a large crater. The crater is often filled with a lake or the sea.

Carbon dioxide (CO_2)   A naturally occurring gas within the Earth's atmosphere. Extra CO_2 due to human activity has contributed about half of global warming.

Case study   Detailed information about real places and real people that explains a geographical idea.

Centralised   Where power is held by a few people in the capital city.

Chlorofluorocarbon (CFC)   A chemical used in some aerosols and fridges which damages the Earth's ozone layer.

Collision zone   The area where two continental plates move together and collide.

Communications   Roads, railways and other ways of linking people and places, including telephones and computers.

Communist government   A government which believes in everyone sharing the country's work and property.

Components   The parts that make up something; for example, a car is made up of thousands of different components.

Consumers   People who buy goods or services.

Continental shelf   The shallow part of the sea around a continent.

Deep sea trench   A deep trench or underwater valley formed where continental crust meets oceanic crust.

Democratic government   A government which is voted into office by the people.

Development indicators   Ways in which development is measured.

Ecotourism   Tourism which is in the environment but doesn't damage it.

Epicentre   The point on the ground above the focus of an earthquake where the vibration is greatest.

Exploited   When a natural resource is used by people.

Exports   Goods and services sold by one country to another.

Factor   The reason for something, or something which brings about a result.

Fault   A break in the rocks caused by movements in the Earth's crust.

Focus   The point beneath the Earth's crust where an earthquake starts.

Fold mountains   Mountains formed by huge pressures in the Earth's crust which push the rocks upwards.

Foreshocks   Small earthquake shocks which come before the main earthquake. They can help warn people of a coming earthquake.

Greenhouse effect   A natural process where carbon dioxide in the atmosphere prevents some of the Earth's heat from escaping back into space. It keeps the Earth warm enough to live on.

Hazard shaking map   A map to show the areas at risk from earthquakes.

Head office   The headquarters of a company, where the company's top bosses work.

Honeypot site   Tourist attraction which attracts many visitors, especially during public holidays and the summer months.

Imports Goods and services that are brought in from another country through trade.

Indicator species Creatures which are very sensitive to pollution. If these creatures are found in water they can show the level of pollution there.

Inequalities Where people are not equal, for example, between rich and poor.

Interdependent People or countries who depend on each other.

Invest To put money into a business.

Kanji A type of Japanese writing.

Lava Molten rock which flows onto the surface of the Earth from an erupting volcano.

Magma Molten rock formed deep beneath the surface of the Earth.

Mainshock The biggest shock of an earthquake.

Manufacturers Companies or people who make goods.

Market The place where goods are sold; for example, the main market for Rover cars is in Britain and the rest of Europe.

Media Newspapers, TV and radio altogether.

Methane (CH_4) A gas produced by industry, car exhausts and cattle. It is a more powerful greenhouse gas than carbon dioxide.

Mid oceanic ridge A long narrow line of underwater mountains, formed in the centre of an ocean by volcanic activity.

Monitor To check or observe something at regular intervals to see if there are any changes. In earthquake areas, for example, scientists use seismographs to detect the first signs of ground movement.

Multinational companies Large companies which operate in many countries around the world.

Nutrients Food for plants or animals; nutrients are absorbed to help plants and animals survive and grow.

Open policy The Chinese government's decision to open up China to foreign trade and investment.

Ozone (O_3) A gas found in the upper layers of the Earth's atmosphere. The ozone layer filters out harmful radiation from the Sun.

Particulates Tiny specks of dust that can form the centre around which raindrops form.

Perceptions How we see or think about something or somebody.

Plateau A large, fairly flat area of highland.

Plate margins The boundary between two tectonic plates.

Prefecture A local government area in Japan, similar to a county in Britain

Shield volcano A volcano that has a broad base and gently sloping sides. It erupts lava flows and fountains that are very 'runny'. An example of a shield volcano is Mauna Loa, Hawaii.

Strait A narrow strip of water between two pieces of land.

Strato volcano A volcano which is made up of layers of lava and ash, built up over many eruptions.

Sustainable tourism Tourism which doesn't damage the environment or people's lifestyles.

Sweatshop A factory where people have to work very long hours, often in difficult or dangerous conditions, for low wages.

Technopole A French centre for science and high-tech industry.

Tectonic plates The Earth's crust is made up of huge slabs called tectonic plates.

Thermal pollution A rise in the temperature of water caused by waste water from factories or power stations.

Trade Buying, selling or exchanging goods, often between countries.

Trading partners Two or more countries who trade together.

Transnational Corporations (TNCs) Large companies that operate in many countries around the world.

Index